TRUTH
Antidote for Error

ANTHONY D. PALMA

GOSPEL PUBLISHING HOUSE
SPRINGFIELD, MISSOURI

02-0904

© 1977 by the Gospel Publishing House, Springfield, Missouri 65802.
All rights reserved. Adapted from *Questions You Will Meet*, by Donald
F. Johns and published by the Gospel Publishing House, © 1964.
Library of Congress Catalog Card Number 76-52177
ISBN 0-88243-904-9. Printed in the United States of America.

A teacher's guide for group study with this book is available from
the Gospel Publishing House (order number 32-0174).

Contents

Contents

1
What Is Truth?

What a wide variety of strange beliefs exists among people who call themselves Christians! Here are some examples: Jesus Christ is no more God than you or I. Living Christians can be baptized on behalf of dead people who were not Christians before they died. Sin and death do not exist; they are merely mistakes of our "mortal mind." We ought to pray to deceased godly people who have been designated as "saints." Once a person is saved, he can never be lost even if he tries to deny the Lord Jesus Christ. The wicked dead are not punished eternally; they are annihilated. Because Jesus died for all men, this means that eventually all men will be saved.

Doctrines of Devils

Listen to what the apostle Paul says about the last days: "Now the Spirit speaketh expressly, that in the latter times some shall depart from the faith, giving heed to seducing spirits, and doctrines of devils; speaking lies in hypocrisy; having their conscience seared with a hot iron" (1 Timothy 4:1,2).

False prophets existed in New Testament times (1 John 4:1), and Jesus warned that in the end time many other false prophets would also arise (Matthew 24:11,24). Satan certainly knows that the coming of the Lord is near, after which he will be judged.

Therefore, he is putting forth extra effort to deceive as many of God's people as possible.

Much of this work of Satan is done through the cults. As we use the term, a *cult* is a religious group that claims to be Christian but whose teachings violate basic Christian beliefs. Cultism, in short, is "any major deviation from orthodox Christianity relative to the cardinal doctrines of the Christian faith" (Walter R. Martin, *The Rise of the Cults* [Grand Rapids: Zondervan Publishing House, 1955], p. 12). The cults will often take one element of Christian truth and distort it.

The cults are a genuine threat to the Church. The Word of God tells us we must "earnestly contend for the faith which was once delivered unto the saints" (Jude 3). One estimate is that as high as 90 percent of the membership of the cults has come from traditional Christian churches. Most of the cults are extremely active in seeking converts. We are all familiar with the door-to-door visitation programs of the Jehovah's Witnesses and the Mormons. We also know that some of the major cults are experiencing a rapid increase in membership.

Some religious groups that are not usually called cults contain basic errors in their doctrinal teachings. Seventh-Day Adventism is basically evangelical in its doctrine, but it also includes a few teachings that are not in accordance with the clear teaching of Scripture—such as the "investigative judgment" and the annihilation of the wicked dead (more on these doctrines later in this book). The Roman Catholic Church is not usually classified as a cult, but some of its teachings also are not in agreement with Scripture—like the idea of purgatory and praying to the "saints."

We must also consider certain groups that are influenced by oriental religions such as Buddhism and

Hinduism, but do not profess to be Christian. Nevertheless, they often draw their members from people who are identified with some Christian church.

Remedy for Error

The only remedy for wrong doctrine is sound doctrine. The only antidote for doctrines of devils is sound doctrine (1 Timothy 1:10; 2 Timothy 4:3; Titus 1:9; 2:1). The teaching and understanding of sound doctrine is of primary importance if we wish to be effective in combating error and in helping those who have fallen into error.

The Authority of the Scriptures

My own conversion to the Lord Jesus came as a result of searching the Scriptures. As a Roman Catholic boy, I did not have the opportunity to read the Bible. In those days the Bible was not made available to Roman Catholics by their church. When my family came in contact with an evangelical woman who witnessed about the Lord Jesus Christ, I became interested. Over a period of months I asked questions concerning basic teachings of the Roman Catholic Church and whether they agreed with the Scriptures. I was satisfied that some of the doctrines I had been taught could not be proved by the Scriptures. I learned and experienced that the only way to be saved was to repent of my sins and trust in the finished work of the Cross.

Not too long after other members of my family and I were converted, we were visited by two Jehovah's Witnesses. We did not know at the time who they were or what they believed. We were simply overjoyed that here were other people who were sharing the Word of God with others. We invited them in and listened to what they said. Fortunately,

7

we detected even at such an early stage that some of their doctrines were false. Consequently, we did not invite them back. Yet it is so easy for Christians today to think that all that is necessary is a belief in the Bible.

These religious groups that have teachings contrary to Scripture do not all have the same view of the Bible. We may classify them in five ways.

1. *The Bible is the only authority.* Both Jehovah's Witnesses and Seventh-Day Adventists insist that the Bible alone is the final authority. They consider it to be the inspired Word of God. Jehovah's Witnesses are very insistent that they believe and teach only what the Bible says. Most of their literature is full of quotations from Scripture. Seventh-Day Adventism likewise insists that the Bible is the only basis for their teachings.

The position of these two groups is very much like the position held by evangelical Christians who teach that the Bible is the inspired Word of God and is the only rule to be followed in matters of doctrine and practice. Yet there is a basic difference between the evangelical view and the view of the Jehovah's Witnesses and the Seventh-Day Adventists. Many Seventh-Day Adventists consider Mrs. Ellen G. White, their founder, to be a prophetess. Jehovah's Witnesses insist that the Bible can be rightly understood only when a person reads their literature explaining it. They are well-known for the considerable amount of printed material that comes off their presses.

2. *The Bible and some other literature are the authority.* While serving on Naval Reserve duty one summer, I engaged in conversation with a fine Mormon young man. He asked what my source of authority was for my beliefs. I responded, "The Bible, which is the inspired Word of God."

8

He commended me, but then proceeded to tell me why the Bible alone is not a sufficient authority. He insisted that we need at least one other book alongside the Bible—*the Book of Mormon.* He tried to illustrate this by saying that if a person drives a nail through a board into a wooden floor, the board can still be shifted. But if another nail is driven through the board, then the board will not move. Consequently, he said, we need both the Bible and the Book of Mormon if we want our faith to be immovable.

Here are some statements that indicate the Mormon position on the Bible: "We believe the Bible to be the Word of God, as far as it is translated correctly; we also believe the Book of Mormon to be the Word of God" (Joseph Smith, *Articles of Faith,* Article 8).

Christian Scientists claim to accept the Bible as their authority, but they too insist we must have an explanatory book alongside it. This book was written by Mary Baker Eddy, the founder of Christian Science, and is called *Science and Health With Key to the Scriptures.* In a Christian Science Sunday morning service, the procedure is to have two readers. One person will read a passage from the Bible, which will be followed by another person reading an explanatory passage from *Science and Health.* Then the process is often repeated. In other words, we cannot understand the Bible without Mrs. Eddy's book!

3. *The Bible and tradition are the final authority.* The Roman Catholic Church officially believes in the Bible as the inspired Word of God. But alongside the authority of the Bible it places the authority of tradition. By tradition, the Roman Catholic Church means the teachings of the Church as they have evolved through the centuries. These teachings, it says, have come through the guidance of the Holy Spirit

9

and the teaching authority of the Church. It also says that the Bible and tradition are not two separate authorities, but that tradition simply expounds what was either explicitly stated in Scripture or implied.

Because of this position, the Roman Catholic Church insists that doctrines such as the sinlessness of Mary, her immaculate conception (that she herself was born without sin), and her bodily ascension into heaven must be accepted just as much as doctrines concerning the Trinity, the virgin birth of Jesus, and the resurrection of Jesus from the dead. These official teachings are called *dogmas*. Any Roman Catholic who rejects a dogma of the Church runs the risk of being excommunicated.

But the Bible itself teaches that in it we have all that we need to know to receive eternal life (John 20:31). Furthermore, some teachings of the Roman Catholic Church are clearly against the teachings of Scripture. We shall see more of this in the following lessons, but we can illustrate it by the Roman Catholic doctrine of purgatory. According to this teaching, very few Christians go directly to heaven when they die. Most of them, because they did not die completely free from sin, must spend time in purgatory—a place that purges or cleanses them of their imperfections and makes them fit for heaven.

How contrary to the Scripture this is! Jesus said that the person who hears His Word and believes on Him already has everlasting life, "and shall not come into condemnation; but is passed from death unto life" (John 5:24).

The history of this whole matter is that whenever any authority is placed alongside the authority of the Bible, eventually the authority of the Bible is weakened and distorted.

4. *The Bible is no special authority at all.* This says that the Bible is simply a book produced by fallible men that gives us their ideas about God. It is not inspired by the Holy Spirit; therefore, we are free to criticize it as much as we want. We may gain some benefit from it, but we are under no obligatior to accept it as authoritative in matters pertaining to our beliefs and practices.

This view is held in modernist-liberal circles. The most outstanding example of this kind of thinking in any church group is the Unitarian-Universalist association.

This view of the Bible exalts human reason. It refuses to admit that because of sin we are not able to make spiritual judgments on our own and therefore need the guidance of God's authoritative Word.

5. *The Bible is no better than any other religious book.* This is similar to the preceding view, but it is held by false teachers who make no claim to being Christians. It is the view held by many of the adherents of the Eastern religions that have influenced thousands in this country. According to them, the Bible may have some value but it is no better than the Moslem Koran or the sacred books of Hinduism and Buddhism.

At this point we must say that the Bible ought to speak for itself. It presents to us God's marvelous redemptive plan for mankind. Those who accept its message about the Lord Jesus Christ know that they have experienced eternal life and are no longer on a spiritual quest. Furthermore, the God whom Christians serve is a personal God (as we shall see in chapter 2), not the kind of God or gods found in oriental religions.

Principles of Interpreting the Bible

Many who say they believe in the Bible are guilty of false doctrine because they do not know how to interpret the Bible. In this section we want to look at some basic rules that will help us in interpreting a passage of Scripture properly.

We will do this by stating the rule and then illustrating it by some false interpretation.

1. *Interpret literally whenever possible.* This means that we must understand words and sentences in Scripture in the usual, normal, and customary way in which they are used. We are not to look for some mysterious meaning.

For instance, Christian Science denies the virgin birth of Jesus. Instead, it interprets the passages that talk about the Virgin Birth in a very obscure way. Mrs. Eddy says: "The Virgin-mother conceived this idea of God, and gave to her ideal the name of Jesus—that is, Joshua, or Savior" (*Science and Health*, p. 334). In another publication we find these words: "Jesus, the Galilean prophet, was born of the Virgin Mary's spiritual thoughts of life and its manifestation" (The First Church of Christ, *Scientist and Miscellany*, p. 261).

In other words, Christian Science rejects the plain language of Scripture which says that Jesus was physically conceived by Mary when the Holy Spirit overshadowed her.

2. *Recognize that sometimes the Bible uses symbolism to explain spiritual truth.* For instance, many passages seem to say that God has a physical body like ours. The Bible talks about the "arm of the Lord," "the eyes of the Lord," "the hand of God." Partly because of this, Mormonism teaches that God has flesh and bones. But the obvious purpose of a phrase

like "the arm of the Lord" is to speak of the power of God in terms we can relate to our own human experience. The arm suggests strength. In a very wonderful way the Bible takes abstract thoughts and illustrates them in language we can understand. This kind of language is called an *anthropomorphism,* which means speaking about God as though He had the form of a man.

3. *The Bible uses figures of speech to help us understand spiritual truth.* One of the most common figures of speech is a metaphor. A metaphor likens one thing to another different thing by speaking of it as if it were that other thing.

At the Last Supper, when Jesus took the bread and wine and said to the disciples, "This is my body," and, "This is my blood." He obviously did not mean that they were literally His body and His blood. He was physically present with them, and with His physical body He was offering them the bread and the wine. The Roman Catholic Church misunderstands these words of Jesus, saying they must be interpreted to mean, "This is my actual, physical body," and, "This is my actual, physical blood."

Figures of speech are so common in the Bible. Remember what the Psalmist says: "The Lord is my Shepherd." This is a metaphor. Certainly it does not mean that the Lord is a literal shepherd with a literal staff in His hand, taking care of literal sheep. When Jesus said, "Ye are the salt of the earth" (Matthew 5:13), He certainly did not mean that His followers are literal salt.

Another illustration of the failure to recognize a figure of speech is in the interpretation given by Jehovah's Witnesses and Seventh-Day Adventists to passages referring to the death of Christians as "sleep" (1 Thessalonians 4:13-15). The interpretation of these two groups is that there is no consciousness after death until the time of the resurrection of the body. They argue that when we go to sleep our minds are unaware of anything that is taking place.

But when the Bible refers to the death of Christians as "sleep," it is simply saying that a deceased Christian is at rest in the Lord. Even modern medical science tells us that while we are asleep our minds can be very active, particularly our subconscious mind. The Bible gives clear teaching that there is consciousness immediately after death. Lazarus the beggar was in Abraham's bosom while the rich man was suffering torment (Luke 16:22-24). To die and be with Christ, Paul says, is far better than to be alive on earth (Philippians 1:23). No, the Bible does not teach the doctrine of soul sleep.

4. *Obscure passages must be interpreted in the light of clear passages.* The Mormons, on the basis of one obscure passage of Scripture, practice proxy baptism. "Else what shall they do which are baptized for the dead, if the dead rise not at all? why are they then baptized for the dead?" (1 Corinthians 15:29). Nowhere else does the Bible ever mention baptism for the dead. Even in this verse, Paul does not say that it is God's will for people to be baptized on behalf of dead people.

Perhaps baptism for the dead was practiced, erroneously, by some misguided people in Paul's day. But the point he is making is that even such people believe in the resurrection from the dead. The topic of that entire chapter is the resurrection from the dead.

5. *A doctrine may not be founded on one verse or a few miscellaneous verses.* The Roman Catholic Church interprets John 20:23 to mean that priests have the authority and power either to forgive sins or to withhold forgiveness. It relates this verse to two others

in Matthew's Gospel. But nowhere do we find in the New Testament that the disciples ever forgave people's sins. Nor do we find the Roman Catholic practice of a person confessing his sins to a priest.

6. *Doctrinal points that cannot be settled by a specific verse or passage may be settled by the general teaching of Scripture.* For instance, the doctrine of the Trinity is not explicity taught in the Bible. Nowhere does the New Testament actually say there are three Persons in the Godhead, and yet these Three are only one God. Because there is no specific statement like that, Jehovah's Witnesses reject the doctrine of the Trinity. Yet a thorough study reveals that the Bible teaches first that there is only one God, and then that the Father is God, the Son is God, and the Holy Spirit is God.

We must come to the conclusion that we cannot, with our limited minds, fully understand everything about God. But some groups insist that they have the complete answer to everything. This is typical of most of the cults. Jehovah's Witnesses deny the doctrine of the Trinity; therefore, they mistranslate passages that unquestionably refer to Jesus as God. The last clause in John 1:1 is properly translated "the Word was God." Yet Jehovah's Witnesses, denying the deity of the Lord Jesus Christ, insist on translating it, "the Word was a god."

2

What Is God Like?

Have you ever heard someone say, "That person is in a class all by himself"? The meaning is that no one is quite like him. Well, this is certainly true about God. Nobody, and nothing, in this world is like Him.

Mankind is incurably religious. Wherever we go on the face of this earth, men worship God or some substitute for God. In this chapter we will examine the common, erroneous ideas about God that some people hold, and what the Bible says about those ideas.

Atheism or Theism?

Atheists say there is no God. The word *atheism* is borrowed from the Greek language. The prefix *a* means "no" and the word *theism* means a belief in deity.

The Bible does not defend the existence of God. It simply starts out: "In the beginning God created the heaven and the earth" (Genesis 1:1). In fact, the atheist is given an unflattering designation when the Bible says: "The fool hath said in his heart, There is no God" (Psalm 14:1).

Atheists often say that the idea of God is contrary to reason, but the Bible says that rejection of the idea of God is contrary to reason. The apostle Paul tells us that God's eternal power and divine nature can be clearly seen in the Creation around us (Romans 1:20).

In the world today, communists are the largest single group of professed atheists. The official philosophy of communism is called *dialectical materialism.* By calling itself materialistic, it denies the priority or existence of anything beyond this world as we know it. The word *dialectical* expresses the idea that communism will ultimately triumph in the world as a result of a series of clashes in history.

Communism is really an ideology that does not express an explicit belief in God, but it does say that some mysterious force is at work in history to insure the triumph of communism. This comes very close to the Christian and Biblical idea that God is in control of the affairs of this world and that His kingdom will ultimately triumph. Communism has a god after all!

Man did not invent the idea of God; God created man with the capacity and yearning to reach out beyond himself to God. This is part of what it means to be made in the image of God (Genesis 1:26).

To Know or Not to Know?

Can we be sure of the existence of God? The agnostic answers, "I don't know." Sometimes agnostics will say that it is impossible to know whether God exists. (The word *agnostic* comes from a Greek word meaning "unable to know.")

Acts 17:23 tells us about an altar in Athens that was dedicated "TO THE UNKNOWN GOD." The Greeks of that day worshiped many gods, but they still felt there might be another God unknown to them or one God above all their other gods.

The Bible contradicts agnosticism. The world of nature that constantly surrounds us testifies to the existence of God (Romans 1:20; Acts 14:15,17). The Psalmist says: "The heavens declare the glory of God; and the firmament showeth his handiwork"

17

(Psalm 19:1). Jesus himself said it is possible to know the only true God (John 17:3). In fact, the entire Bible has been given to us that we might not be in doubt about the existence of God and that we might come to know Him in a personal way through Jesus Christ.

The Cosmic Clock Winder

Deism was a popular belief among intellectuals at the time the United States was founded. Unlike atheism and agnosticism, deism believes in the existence of God and that He created the universe. But it then teaches that God completely detached himself from the universe after He created it. This belief may be illustrated by imagining God to be a clockmaker. After making the clock, He wound it up and then left it alone. In other words, according to deism God has withdrawn himself from all contact with His universe.

Deism can be commended for teaching that God is the Creator of the universe and that He is distinct from it and greater than it (in contrast to pantheism, which we will discuss next). But its view of God is that He is totally detached from any interest in His creation, including mankind.

According to the Bible, God still gives "to all life, and breath, and all things" and "in him we live, and move, and have our being" (Acts 27:25,28). The apostle Paul tells us, concerning Jesus Christ, that He not only participated in the creation of our world, but "in Him all things hold together" (Colossians 1:17, *NASB*).

Deism's God is very impersonal. But the God of the Bible takes a strong personal interest in us. He is not only the great cosmic Creator, He is also the Redeemer. He is so concerned about us that He sent His Son to this world to redeem it (John 3:16).

God Is Nature—Nature Is God

Deism stresses the transcendence of God—that He is completely separate from His creation. *Pantheism* is the opposite. It teaches that God is all, and all is God. In other words, God is not distinct from His creation. Spiritism (spiritualism) seems to have this view of God. It is the view held by many oriental religious groups. Theosophy, which is strongly influenced by Hinduism, teaches that God is an impersonal principle that permeates the universe. Hindu and Buddhist thought (including religious groups in the United States that owe their origin to these two religions) is basically pantheistic.

Pantheism eliminates the distinction between man and God. Sometimes pantheists speak of God as being in all mankind.

God is indeed everywhere present. This is often referred to as divine immanence. Jeremiah was aware of this when he wrote: "Do not I fill heaven and earth? saith the Lord" (Jeremiah 23:24).

The Bible teaches both the transcendence of God and His omnipresence. He is different from His creation, but at the same time He is still very much interested in His creation.

A Physical Being?

Joseph Smith, the founder of Mormonism, taught that "the Father has a body of flesh and bones as tangible as man's" (*Doctrine and Covenants*, [Salt Lake City: Church of Jesus Christ of Latter-day Saints], CXXX, 22; CXXXI, 7). Nowhere does the Bible teach this. Jesus plainly said, "God is spirit" (John 4:24, *NASB*). A valid translation would also be, "God

19

is a spirit." But in either case, Jesus emphasized that God's essential nature is spirit; He is a spirit-being. By definition, a spirit does not have a body, although spirits may inhabit bodies.

Of course, the Bible often uses human physical terms to describe some of God's activities. We read often about the "arm of the Lord" or the "eye of the Lord." Expressions like this help us, with our limited ability to grasp eternal truth, to understand something about God by using terms familiar to us. The arm signifies strength; the eyes signify awareness. If God indeed had a physical body, He could not possibly be present everywhere (Psalm 139:7-18).

Unseen by Human Eye

God is often spoken of as being invisible (Romans 1:20; Colossians 1:15; 1 Timothy 1:17; Hebrews 11:27). The human eye can never see God; it can only see manifestations of His presence and power.

A Russian cosmonaut, upon returning from a space trip, was asked if he had seen God up there. He replied, "No." How different from some American astronauts who upon their return to earth testified to a greater awareness of God! Yet neither the Russian nor the Americans had actually seen God himself with their physical eyes.

A mother asked her young daughter what she was drawing. The child replied, "A picture of God." "But no one knows what God looks like," said the mother. The child replied, "They will when I get through!"

But God has indeed given us a very lucid and beautiful picture of himself. John 1:18 tells us: "No man hath seen God at any time," but it goes on to say that God's only begotten Son "hath declared [explained] him." When Philip said to Jesus, "Lord, show us the Father, and it is enough for us," Jesus responded by saying: "He who has seen Me has seen the Father; how do you say, 'Show us the Father'?" (John 14:8,9, *NASB*).

Three, Yet One

There is only one God. This truth is constantly emphasized in the Old Testament, and is what distinguished ancient Israel from all her pagan neighbors. "Hear, O Israel: The LORD our God is one LORD" (Deuteronomy 6:4). The Old Testament also reiterates the statement that there is no one else beside God (4:35). We find the same teaching in the New Testament (see Mark 12:29; 1 Corinthians 8:4; 1 Timothy 2:5).

He's One, Not Many

Monotheism, the belief in only one God, is directly opposed to polytheism, a belief in many gods. Animism is one form of polytheism. This belief is quite common among primitive people. It teaches that the world is filled with spirits (or gods) and these spirits animate, or give life to, the objects in which they dwell. The spirits may dwell in rocks, trees, rivers, hills, or anywhere.

Polytheism often takes the form of idolatry. Idolatry is the worship of images that represent gods. When Paul went to Athens, his spirit was agitated because of the many idols he saw.

Polytheism is a direct violation of the first commandment which says: "Thou shalt have no other gods before me" (Exodus 20:3). The whole Bible refutes the idea that there are many gods. Paul wrote: "We know that an idol is nothing in the world, and that there is none other God but one" (1 Corinthians 8:4). The Bible does teach that other spirits are in the

21

world, but it emphatically states that there is only one God.

Mormonism directly contradicts the Biblical teaching of monotheism. It maintains that many gods exist and that these gods are human beings grown divine. Brigham Young, an early Mormon leader, said: "And you have got to learn how to be Gods yourself the same as all Gods have done before you." He called Adam the God of this world and said that Adam "is our Father and our God, and the only God with whom we have to do" (Brigham Young, *Journal of Discourses,* Romans 6:4; Romans 1:50).

Christianity is not unique in teaching the existence of only one God. Judaism, Islam, and Sikhism all teach the existence of only one God. The unique element in the Christian and Biblical view of God is that within this unity three Persons exist. The Lord said: "Let us make man in *our* image, after *our* likeness" (Genesis 1:26).

In the New Testament, this triunity of God is very apparent at the time of Jesus' baptism. As Jesus came up out of the water, the Holy Spirit descended like a dove, and the Father's voice spoke from heaven (Matthew 3:16,17). Jesus himself commanded that believers be baptized in the name of the Father, Son, and Holy Spirit (Matthew 28:19). Furthermore, Paul speaks of the love of God, the grace of the Lord Jesus Christ, and the fellowship of the Holy Spirit (2 Corinthians 13:14).

It is impossible for anyone to understand fully the Biblical doctrine of the Trinity. We must content ourselves with accepting the Biblical teaching first that God is One, and then that He exists in three Persons. But Christians do not worship three gods; they worship the triune God.

Three main groups oppose this doctrine of the Trinity. The Unitarians and many liberal groups regard Jesus as simply a man. Consequently, He could not be a member of the Godhead any more than any other human being can. They believe Jesus is not divine any more than any other human being is capable of being divine.

Jehovah's Witnesses are probably the most vocal opponents of the doctrine of the Trinity. According to them, Jehovah of the Old Testament is the only God. Jesus is "a god" who was the first created being in the universe. Consequently, He could not be equal to Jehovah God.

This teaching of the Jehovah's Witnesses is flatly contradicted by Scripture. "For in him [Christ] dwelleth all the fullness of the Godhead bodily" (Colossians 2:9). The correct translation of John 1:1, as any reputable scholar will say, is: "The Word was God," not, "The Word was a god," as Jehovah's Witnesses insist. Furthermore, Philippians 2:6,7 clearly says that Jesus was and is equal with God.

A third group opposing the doctrine of the Trinity is part of the Pentecostal Movement. Those who hold this teaching are often referred to as "Oneness" or "Jesus Only" people. They teach that there is only one Person in the Godhead, whose full name is Lord Jesus Christ. The Father and the Holy Spirit are viewed as manifestations of Jesus. This teaching denies that there are three Persons in the Godhead, and prefers to think of the Father, Son, and Holy Spirit as different ways or modes in which God manifests himself.

It is extremely difficult to understand how a distinction of Persons in the Godhead can be denied. To whom did Jesus pray, if it was not Someone other than himself?

Is God's Knowledge Limited?

A clear teaching of Scripture is that God knows everything. He is omniscient. He knows not only everything that has taken place in the past, but also everything that is presently taking place and that will take place. The abundance of predictive prophecies in the Bible demonstrates that God knows all about the future.

In our day some are teaching a doctrine of conditional foreknowledge. They maintain that God does not know *everything* about the future. The argument is advanced that if God did indeed know everything, including all of our future acts, this would strip us of free will. To put it another way, if God knows what your decisions and actions will be tomorrow, this means you have no choice regarding those decisions or actions because they must necessarily come to pass.

We must understand that God is not bound by time as we understand it. The Lord is the I AM (Exodus 3:14). With Him there is no past or future. The fact that He knows something will come to pass does not necessarily mean He predetermined it should happen that way. It simply means that being God, He is aware of all alternatives and contingencies and always knows exactly how events will turn out.

3

Do Evil and Good Spirits Exist?

Is there really a spirit world? Apart from God, are there other spirits in this universe? Are there unseen personalities in the world—some good, some bad—who have a bearing on our lives?

The answers vary. Some groups believe in the existence of God but reject the idea of a personal devil and other spirit beings. Others try to explain certain happenings in terms of impersonal forces in the universe. Still others reject completely any idea of any spirit beings, including God. But what does the Bible say?

Satan Is a Reality

Perhaps the greatest achievement of the devil is to convince people he does not exist. After all, Jesus did call him a liar (John 8:44).

We do not need to probe too deeply into Scripture to see that Satan is a person. The account of the temptation of Jesus in the wilderness is sufficient to demonstrate this (Matthew 4:1-11). Jesus engaged in actual conversation with the devil. The devil is a rational being. He tempted Jesus in a very subtle way.

But Satan was not always this way. When we read Ezekiel 28:11-19 we know the prophet is speaking concerning the King of Tyrus. But many believe this man was also a type of Satan. He is referred to, for instance, as "the anointed cherub that covereth" (v. 14). It is said of him: "Thou wast perfect in thy ways from the day that thou wast created, till iniquity was found in thee" (v. 15). Isaiah's denunciation of the king of Babylon also suggests that he may have had Satan in mind (Isaiah 14:12-15). In this passage, pride was the cause of Satan's fall. And from the time of his fall, he has sinned continually. "The devil sinneth from the beginning" (1 John 3:8).

The names given to Satan reveal something about his nature. He is called the wicked one (Matthew 13:19), Belial or vileness (2 Corinthians 6:15), the devil or slanderer (Matthew 4:1), Satan or adversary (Zechariah 3:1; 1 Peter 5:8), Abaddon or perdition (Revelation 9:11), Apollyon or destroyer (Revelation 9:11). He is called a murderer (John 8:44), a liar (John 8:44), that old serpent (Revelation 12:9).

In addition to all this, he is "the prince of this world" (John 12:31; 14:30; 16:11), "the prince of the power of the air" (Ephesians 2:2), and "the god of this world [age]" (2 Corinthians 4:4).

He's Busy All the Time

The Bible gives many details concerning the activities of Satan. The following are some of the main ones:

1. *He tempts.* God does not tempt (James 1:13), but he does permit Satan to tempt us at times (1 Thessalonians 3:5), even though these temptations are not so great that we will not be able to overcome them (1 Corinthians 10:13).

2. *He lies.* Jesus said: "There is no truth in him. When he speaketh a lie, he speaketh of his own: for he is a liar, and the father of it" (John 8:44). He is

cunning and deceptive (Ephesians 6:11; 2 Corinthians 2:11), and is even able to transform himself into a messenger or angel of light (2 Corinthians 11:14). In his relationships with men, this started in the garden of Eden when he said to Eve: "Ye shall not surely die" (Genesis 3:4).

3. *He blinds people spiritually.* The apostle Paul said:"The god of this world hath blinded the minds of them which believe not, lest the light of the glorious gospel of Christ, who is the image of God, should shine unto them" (1 Corinthians 4:4).

4. *He afflicts both God's people and sinners.* He may afflict believers only with God's permission (Job 1: 6-12; 2:1-6). He also oppresses and possesses ungodly people (Acts 10:38).

5. *He falsely accuses.* He is called the accuser of the brethren (Revelation 12:10). He delights in bringing Christians under a sense of condemnation.

6. *He fights against God's people* (Ephesians 6: 11-16). He seeks to hinder God's work. Paul said in one place, "Satan hindered us" (1 Thessalonians 2:18).

7. *He is responsible for false doctrines.* These are called "doctrines of devils [demons]" (1 Timothy 4:1).

Christians and the Devil

Christians must not permit Satan to gain an advantage over them. They must be sober and vigilant and must resist him (1 Peter 5:8; Ephesians 4:27; James 4:7). They must put on the whole armor of God to be able to stand against him (Ephesians 6:11).

Satan is a defeated enemy. The promise of this goes back to Genesis 3:15 when God said to the serpent: "I will put enmity between thee and the woman, and between thy seed and her seed; it shall bruise thy head, and thou shalt bruise his heel."

Jesus accomplished this by dying on the cross. He died, "that through death he might destroy him that had the power of death, that is, the devil" (Hebrews 2:14). The eternal destiny of the devil is to be cast into the lake of fire and brimstone and to be tormented day and night for ever and ever (Revelation 20:10).

In view of all this, we do not need to fear Satan. He is really a coward, and if we resist him he will flee from us (James 4:7). How can we resist the devil? What better example do we have than the Lord Jesus Christ?

In the account of the temptation of Jesus in the wilderness (Matthew 4:1-11), two things stand out. The first is that Jesus was led by the Spirit (v. 1). The best way to fight Satan, the evil spirit, is with the Holy Spirit. Prior to this incident, Jesus had just been baptized and the Spirit of God had descended upon Him. It is important to be filled with the Holy Spirit to combat Satan successfully.

A second point is that Jesus knew the Word of God and used it very effectively. Satan, being a liar, twisted the Scriptures to suit his own purposes. But Jesus responded by a correct use of the Word of God in each instance.

It is unfortunate that some people have no fear whatever of Satan. In the United States we now have satanist churches. The members openly admit they worship Satan. It seems they have given themselves over to him completely.

Erroneous Views About Satan

Zoroastrianism, the religion of ancient Persia, taught

that two great spiritual and eternal beings are at war. Both existed from the very beginning. Ahura Mazda represents the good. Angra Mainyu represents the evil. Ahura Mazda will triumph in the end and will banish his evil counterpart to the regions from which he came.

This concept of an eternal dualism has sometimes found its way into the Church. But the Bible teaches that Satan is a created being, not an eternal being. In Colossians 1:16 we read that Christ was the Agent in the creation of all spirit beings (referred to as thrones, dominions, principalities, and powers). Some of these are identified with the forces of wickedness (Ephesians 6:12).

Christian Science teaches that the devil exists only as a lie in someone's mind. Like sin and death, the devil is an error of "Mortal Mind." But we have already seen that the devil is more than a lie in someone's mind. He is actually a liar himself (John 8:44). The teaching of Christian Science is very close to the idea of many non-Christian scientists—that the devil does not really exist. But Satan is subtle and deceitful, and if he can convince people that he is only a wrong thought, they will fall into his snare (1 Timothy 3:7; 2 Timothy 2:26).

The Unity School of Christianity holds a view of Satan similar to that of Christian Science. For Unity, the devil is an adverse state of consciousness that permits the lying thought to find lodging. Satan is not a person, but instead is a person's mind allowing a wrong thought to exist.

We have already seen that Satan is a person, and not simply a thought. He is a person who blinds the minds of sinful men (2 Corinthians 4:4). One result of this intellectual blindness is that men will come up with wrong ideas about him.

Spiritism denies the existence of either a personal God or a personal devil. It teaches that spirits do exist, but they are only departed human spirits. We have already dealt with this view in our discussion of the personality of Satan.

Is Satan Always Responsible?

When we read the account of the temptation of Adam and Eve in the garden of Eden, we know that Satan was responsible for the entrance of sin into the world. But is he always responsible for specific sins we commit?

I remember so clearly an incident that happened in our Sunday school many years ago. It was a small Sunday school, and the superintendent was a strict disciplinarian. Sometimes she wanted to know why we were late for Sunday school. On one occasion a very young girl, perhaps 6 years old, was asked by the superintendent why she was late. The child immediately responded, "The devil made me late."

Some people, upon being confronted with sins they have committed, immediately respond, "The devil made me do it." This attitude relieves them of all responsibility for sin. The devil does indeed tempt God's people, but in the final analysis God holds us responsible for any sins we commit. "But every man is tempted, when he is drawn away of his own lust, and enticed" (James 1:14). Yet God is faithful; He will not allow us to be tempted beyond our endurance (1 Corinthians 10:13).

We know too that along with the entrance of sin into the world, sickness also made its appearance. But can we say that the devil is directly responsible for all sickness in the world today?

Of course, the Bible does teach that some sickness is caused by Satan. Concerning the woman who had an infirmity for 18 years and whom Jesus healed, the Lord said that Satan had bound her all those years (Luke 13:16). But sometimes sicknesses come because of our failure to observe the basic laws of good health. If I do not eat nourishing food and get proper rest, I cannot blame Satan for my body's lowered resistance to sickness and disease. If I expose myself to a contagious disease, I cannot blame Satan if I contract that disease.

Nevertheless, God is more concerned with the cure for sickness than with its cause. The Lord Jesus healed all people of their sicknesses, whether or not Satan was the cause.

Do Demons Exist?

A person's attitude toward believing in the devil carries over to his attitude toward demons. Who or what are demons? Many Biblical scholars identify demons with the host of angels who followed Lucifer in his rebellion against God, and consequently were cast out of heaven. These fallen angels work along with Satan in carrying out his plans (Matthew 25:41; Revelation 12:7-12).

The work of these evil angels falls into the following categories:

1. *They inflict diseases* (Matthew 9:33; 12:22; Luke 9:37-42). Sometimes this is in the form of demon possession.

2. *They are responsible for some false doctrines* (1 Timothy 4:1). Sometimes demons pose as good angels. Even Satan sometimes comes as an angel of light (2 Corinthians 11:14).

31

3. *They try to separate a believer from his Lord* (Romans 8:38). In the Epistles we sometimes read about thrones, dominions, principalities, and powers. Biblical scholars generally agree that these refer to angelic beings, and often to fallen angels.

A child of God does not fear demons. The atoning work of Jesus on the cross defeated Satan and all his angels. As we abide in Christ, we can rest assured that spiritual victory will always be ours.

But can a believer be demon possessed? Unfortunately, some are teaching that this is possible. But the Bible nowhere teaches this. Only those who do not have Christ in their hearts can be possessed by demons. As we shall see in a future chapter, all Christians have the indwelling Holy Spirit. God simply will not allow evil spirits to dwell in the same place with His Holy Spirit.

Furthermore, we are told: "Greater is he that is in you, than he that is in the world" (1 John 4:4). When we read the preceding verses, we discover that John is talking about evil spirits.

The Bible talks about three types of demonology. They are given by Henry C. Thiessen in his *Lectures in Systematic Theology* (Grand Rapids: Wm. B. Eerdmans Publishing Co., 1949). The *first* is fortune-telling and astrology. We will deal with these in chapter 9. *Another form* of demonology is spiritism, sometimes incorrectly called spiritualism. Spiritism is the belief that the living can establish contact with the dead, and that the spirits of the dead can communicate with men. *A third form*, and one that sometimes is the result of the preceding one, is demon possession and the direct worship of demons. During the tribulation period demon activity will be renewed and the dragon (Satan) will be openly worshiped (Revelation 16:13,14; 13:4).

In some of the oriental religions that have gained a following in the United States, the devotees are encouraged to meditate a long period of time, sometimes chanting a sacred word over and over again. When people are in this state, they are prime targets for demon possession.

The destiny of evil angels is the same as Satan's. Along with him they will be cast into eternal hell (Matthew 25:41). In the meantime, some of them are being kept in spiritual chains and under darkness (2 Peter 2:4; Jude 6), while others are free to carry out the work of their diabolic master. But when the Lord Jesus Christ returns, believers will have a part in the judgment and condemnation of the evil angels (1 Corinthians 6:3).

An Angel of Light

"Satan himself is transformed into an angel of light" (2 Corinthians 11:14). Satan and his angels do not always present themselves to us in an objectionable form or manner. Satan is the archdeceiver. Throughout the Bible we read about angelic visitations. But any message that seems to come from an angelic being must be evaluated by the Word of God. The apostle Paul was very strong on this point: "But though we, or an angel from heaven, preach any other gospel unto you than that which we have preached unto you, let him be accursed" (Galatians 1:8).

The word *angel*, in both its Hebrew and Greek forms, literally means "messenger." In those languages one word was used with the double meaning of a messenger or an angel. This emphasizes the point that God has used His angels to convey His message to men. But Satan also uses his own angels to deceive men.

One of the best examples of this is found in the experience of Mohammad. Mohammad said he was visited by the angel Gabriel while in a cave. As a result of that visit, Mohammad set about to establish what he believed to be the only true religion. But we know from the history and doctrines of the Moslem religion that it is very far removed from the truth. It was not the angel Gabriel after all. It was some evil angel, perhaps Satan himself, posing as Gabriel.

The same must be said about the establishment of Mormonism. Joseph Smith, the founder of Mormonism, maintained that in 1823 he was visited by an angel whose name was Moroni. The angel revealed to Smith the location of a buried box which contained golden plates in the "reformed Egyptian tongue." Four years later he was permitted to remove the plates and then translated them with the aid of the "Urim and Thummin" provided him by the angel. This became the Book of Mormon.

But the teachings of the Book of Mormon are absolutely contrary to the Word of God. Consequently, the angel who Joseph Smith said visited him could not have been from God. If there was any angelic visitation at all, it was Satan once again posing as an angel of light.

Should Angels Be Worshiped?

We already talked about Satan worship. But is it ever proper to worship the good angels? The Roman Catholic Church includes angels among the many saints to whom prayers are offered. Some prayers are addressed to Michael and Gabriel, the archangels.

God alone is to be worshiped. On two occasions the apostle John fell at the feet of an angel to worship him (Revelation 19:10; 22:8,9). In both cases the angel told him not to do it, but to worship God. Yet it is common practice for Roman Catholics to kneel before a statue of "St. Michael" and offer prayers. They will say that they are not worshiping either the statue or Michael, but that they are praying to him. If this is indeed the case, it still comes dangerously close to what the Scriptures forbid.

4

What Is Sin?

The word *sin* is like the word *die*. Many people are afraid to use either word. Do you refer to a person "passing on," being "no longer with us," or "leaving us"? Are you reluctant to say simply that he died? It's that way with the idea of sin. How many substitutes have you heard for it? We hear people speak of "shortcomings," "weaknesses," and "failings." Even when specific sins are mentioned by name, we often hear expressions like *white* lie or *half*-truth.

The Bible is very forthright in dealing with the question of sin. God is so concerned about helping us solve the problem of sin in our lives that He does not hesitate to call sin by its correct name. It is only when we are willing to identify sin as sin that God is able to help us.

The Origin of Sin

Where did sin originate? The Zoroastrian religion of Persia was quite strong in New Testament times and still exists today under the name of Parsees. It teaches that sin never had an origin. It teaches that good and evil always existed side by side as two eternal principles. This theory is sometimes called an eternal dualism.

As we saw in the preceding chapter, sin had its origin in the rebellion of Lucifer against God. The devil has sinned from the beginning (1 John 3:8).

36

He is the ultimate source of all sin. But remember that Lucifer is a created being and that sin entered the universe some time after God's creation of all the angels.

As far as man is concerned, sin had its origin at the Fall. The sin of Adam was disobedience to God by partaking of the fruit of the tree of the knowledge of good and evil (Genesis 3:1-8; 1 Timothy 2:13,14). Satan was present in the garden of Eden in the form of a serpent which he possessed. He did tempt Eve, who in turn tempted Adam.

Adam blamed Eve, and Eve blamed the serpent (Genesis 3:12,13). But God held them individually responsible. The apostle Paul tells us that as a result of Adam's disobedience, sin entered the world (Romans 5:12). So you see that while the devil is ultimately responsible for the origin of evil, our first parents are responsible for the entrance of sin into this world.

The Nature of Sin

The Bible uses many different words to designate acts of rebellion against God—iniquity, transgression, trespass. But the most comprehensive word it uses is *sin* (Greek, *hamartia*). In its verb form it means "to miss the mark."

The precise meaning of this word is portrayed in Judges 20:16: "Among all this people there were seven hundred chosen men lefthanded; every one could sling stones at a hair breadth, and not *miss*." Sinning, in other words, means missing the target of God's righteous standard. This is the meaning of Romans 3:23 which says: "For all have sinned, and come short of the glory of God."

The Bible gives a few pithy statements that help

us to understand something of the nature of sin. Here are some of them:

Sin is transgression of the Law (1 John 3:4).

All unrighteousness is sin (5:17).

To one who knows to do good and does not do it, to him it is sin (James 4:17).

Whatever is not of faith is sin (Romans 14:23).

How can you determine if an act or thought is sinful? Ask yourself several questions:

1. Does the Bible clearly designate it as a sin? The Scriptures give several catalogs of sins that spell out what is displeasing to God, such as the one in Galatians 5:19-21 that enumerates adultery, fornication, uncleanness, lasciviousness, idolatry, witchcraft, hatred, variance, emulations, wrath, strife, seditions, heresies, envyings, murders, drunkenness, revelings (see also Romans 1:29-32; Mark 7:21-23; 1 Corinthians 6:9,10; James 3).

2. Can you do it in faith to the glory of God in the name of Jesus? The Bible does not list every conceivable sin. Furthermore, though some actions are not clearly designated as sin in Scripture, some believers will not feel free to do them. We are told: "Let every man be fully persuaded in his own mind" (Romans 14:5; also v. 23). In this connection, we must always be sensitive to the leading of the indwelling Holy Spirit. Often an inner unrest will indicate that the Spirit of God is cautioning us against doing a certain thing.

3. Will it cause a brother for whom Christ died to stumble and perish? Even though some activities may be perfectly legitimate on the basis of the two preceding questions, they may not be proper on the basis of this question. An action may not be sinful in itself, but it becomes sinful when it causes someone to stumble spiritually (1 Corinthians 8:11,12).

The Penalty of Sin

The consequences of sin may be given in just one word—*death*. "The soul that sinneth, it shall die" (Ezekiel 18:20). "The wages of sin is death" (Romans 6:23). Death may be thought of in three ways:

1. *Physical death.* The Lord said to Adam: "Unto dust shalt thou return" (Genesis 3:19). It was through Adam that death spread to all men (Romans 5:12). Physical death—the separation of the body from the soul—is the lot of all men and is a very solemn reminder of the far-reaching consequences of sin. But thank God, for us believers even death will be vanquished when we are raised to immortality (1 Corinthians 15:53-57).

2. *Spiritual death.* This has to do with the separation of the spirit from God. When God created man in His image, He endowed him with a spirit by which man could have fellowship with Him. When Adam sinned, that fellowship was disrupted so that Adam hid himself from God. Unredeemed men, refusing to repent of their sin, cannot have fellowship with God. We have access into God's presence only by the Lord Jesus Christ, who shed His blood for our sins (Ephesians 2:18; 3:12).

3. *Eternal death.* This is simply an extension of the previous point. It means eternal separation from the presence of God (Romans 1:32; James 5:20). The Scriptures refer to this as the second death (Revelation 2:11; 20:6,14; 21:8).

The Universality of Sin

The Bible declares that all men are sinners (Romans 3:9-18,23). In Romans 5, Paul says we know sin is universal because of the universality of death. Even before God gave the Law, men were held responsible for their sin. Then after the Law was given, men were responsible for obeying its specific commandments. From the time of Adam until now, all men have been guilty in some way of violating God's will.

Sin is like a spiritual disease that has infected the entire race. The Bible is not specific about the manner in which the sin of Adam affected all mankind, but it does trace our sin to him. It may be best to think of this as our spiritual and moral constitution being adversely affected by the Fall in such a way that we find it much easier to sin than to resist sin. But however the sin of our first parents may have affected us, the Bible is so very clear that we are condemned for our own sins.

The opening chapters of the Book of Romans show us that God will condemn both Gentiles and Jews if they fail to live up to the light He has granted them. The non-Jews, Paul says, still have the revelation of God in nature which talks about His eternal power and divine nature, "so that they are without excuse" (Romans 1:20).

It is only because the Gentiles originally rejected this revelation of God in His creation that they were given over to idolatry and all forms of immorality. Likewise, the Jews who have the Law are also without excuse (2:1) because they have sinned under the Law (v. 12). Because sin is universal, condemnation must also be universal. But God has provided forgiveness and redemption for all mankind through His Son (John 3:16).

False Views About Sin

In this section of the chapter you will learn about some of the major false teachings about the nature of sin.

Christian Science. According to Christian Science, sin is unreal. *Science and Health,* the major work of Mary Baker Eddy, the founder of Christian Science, repeats the phrase "There is no sin." This teaching regards sin and evil as illusions—the product of "Mortal Mind." (But it seems that Christian Science never quite explains what is meant by the expression *mortal mind.*) Sin, it says, is an error of the human mind. "Therefore the only reality of sin, sickness, or death is the awful fact that unrealities seem real to human, erring belief, until God strips off their disguise. They are not true, because they are not of God" (*Science and Health,* p. 472).

But according to the Bible, sin is real. If not, why did Jesus have to die? He died to rescue us from the power, guilt, and reality of sin. "Who his own self bare our sins in his own body on the tree" (1 Peter 2:24).

According to Christian Science, sin is overcome by following the example of Jesus who demonstrated to mankind what affection and goodness really mean by dying on the cross. "Unreal" sin is overcome by replacing it with real love and goodness.

But according to Scripture, it is the actual sacrifice of Jesus on the cross, not His example, that frees us from sin. We were redeemed with His precious blood (1:19). Christian Science is essentially a bloodless religion. We must remember that "without the shedding of blood there is no forgiveness of sins" (Hebrews 9:22, *The Living Bible*).

Unity. Although Unity is similar to Christian Science in many respects, it does admit that sin is real and that sin came into existence with the fall of man. It teaches that this fall was from a higher state of consciousness, so man now exists in a lower mental state or condition.

In other words, sin is the guilt of the carnal mind. We are to deal with it by freeing our carnal mind from the bondage of its lower state of consciousness. This is accomplished by returning to the original higher state of consciousness that man had before the Fall. Whereas Christian Science denies the existence of evil, Unity seems to ignore its presence by teaching that it is only temporary.

According to the Bible, however, the fall of man was moral, not mental. Adam chose to disobey rather than obey God. As a result of that choice, he did not lose knowledge, as Unity teaches, but rather he gained a knowledge of good and evil (see Genesis 2:17; 3:5,7,22).

We cannot gain freedom from sin by substituting high thoughts for low thoughts—what some people would call "positive thinking." Paul said: "For I know that in me (that is, in my flesh,) dwelleth no good thing: for to will is present with me; but how to perform that which is good I find not" (Romans 7:18). We cannot deliver ourselves from sin and its guilt. This deliverance comes only by faith in the crucified and risen Christ.

Mormonism. Mormonism's view of sin is very curious. It teaches that sin is both necessary and appropriate. Even Adam had to sin. By sinning, Adam brought about the possibility of becoming a god (Genesis 3:5,22).

Once again, the Biblical view of sin has been distorted by Mormonism. Nowhere does the Bible teach that it was necessary and desirable for Adam or any other man to sin. Since sin is a violation of the will of God, how can a person possibly become a god by violating God's commandments?

Man was created with the possibility to sin, but also with the possibility not to sin. And it is this latter possibility that was God's will for mankind. Mormonism has made the mistake of teaching that the end justifies the means. In other words, it says that for man (Adam) to become a god he had to violate the will of God.

Unitarian-Universalism. The view of this theologically-liberal denomination is that we are not fallen sinners. Sin is really a defect of human nature and we should not condemn it, any more than we would condemn a physical defect in a person. This group has a very optimistic view of man who, they say, is struggling to overcome his defects. In time, with the help of culture and education, we will succeed in saving ourselves by our own good works.

This view of sin is held not only by this particular group but generally by all those who pride themselves on being theologically liberal. It is often stated in terms of the perfectability of man. At best, Jesus is viewed as the moral example for us to follow, but not as the Redeemer who needed to shed His blood for the cleansing of our sins.

But the Bible teaches that sin is not a defect—it is disobedience. "Every one who practices sin also practices lawlessness; and sin is lawlessness" (1 John 3:4, *NASB*). We have no control over physical defects that are thrust upon us, but sin is something we voluntarily choose to do. We cannot save ourselves, for "a man is not justified by the works of the Law but through faith in Christ Jesus" (Galatians 2:16, *NASB*).

Cultural relativism. Sometimes what is regarded as right in one country is wrong in another. Even within our own country, opinions concerning what is right and what is wrong sometimes vary from one section to another. Because of this we may say that to some extent the rightness or wrongness of certain

43

actions is relative to, or depends upon, the culture of a particular area. From this we get the name *cultural relativism.*

This idea is not new to students of sociology, social psychology, and cultural anthropology. We know there is some truth in it. But a thoroughgoing cultural relativist does not say that the rightness or wrongness of *some* things is relative to culture. He says that the rightness or wrongness of *all* things is relative to culture. This subtle shift from "some" to "all" means that for him nothing is sinful in itself. A thing is sinful only because a particular culture says it is sinful.

You will find cultural relativism to some degree in the New Testament. For example, Paul said: "And unto the Jews I became as a Jew, that I might gain the Jews; to them that are under the law, as under the law, that I might gain them that are under the law; to them that are without law, as without law, (being not without law to God, but under the law to Christ,) that I might gain them that are without law" (1 Corinthians 9:20,21).

The key to understanding this is that in matters where culture did not conflict with his faith, Paul went along with what the culture believed to be right or wrong, so that he could win the lost to Christ.

Paul exemplified this in the matter of eating meat. He refused to eat meat when he thought it might cause someone to stumble, even though he himself knew there was nothing wrong with eating it (1 Corinthians 8:13; Romans 14:15).

Situation ethics. Situation ethics is very similar to extreme cultural relativism. It says that nothing is wrong in itself, but that the particular situation in which we contemplate or execute an action determines whether it is right or wrong.

Situation ethics has no absolute moral standard. It will maintain, for example, that sexual relations outside the marriage bond are not always wrong. According to this view, sometimes it is very helpful for a person to engage in this kind of activity. The same holds true with respect to homosexual acts, lying, stealing, and virtually any other act designated as sin in the Scriptures.

According to the Bible, some actions are sins because they are violations of God's law no matter what the particular situation is. Paul always regarded himself as being under the law of Christ (1 Corinthians 9:21). God's standards of morality are absolute and must not be violated, no matter what a particular culture or specific situation may dictate.

5

How Are We Saved?

The Philippian jailer asked life's most important question: "What must I do to be saved?" (Acts 16:30). Most people know something is wrong in their relationship with God or whatever gods they try to serve. And many want to get right with whatever or whomever they worship.

Non-Christian religions have many answers. Even within Christianity we find a variety of answers. Some think they can be saved by beating their bodies. Others think they can be saved by doing all sorts of "religious" things.

In Rome you can visit La Scala Santa (the Holy Stairs). This is supposed to be the stairway of Pilate's Judgment Hall which was transported to Rome. You will see people going up the stairs on their knees, stopping on each stair to recite some prayers. By this they hope to gain some favor with God.

God's Conditions for Salvation

1. *Repentance*. John the Baptist, Jesus, Peter, and Paul all preached the necessity of repentance (see Matthew 3:2; 4:17; Acts 2:38; 3:19; 17:30; 20:21). The Greek word translated "repentance" means literally "a change of mind or attitude."

Before a person can be saved, he must admit he is a sinner (1 John 1:9). In other words, repentance means that a person changes his thinking about sin. He is genuinely sorry for his sin because it has offended God. This becomes possible only with the help of the Holy Spirit (see John 16:8,9). By repenting, a person not only admits his sin but also determines by God's grace to live a God-pleasing life.

2. *Faith.* We must not only repent, we must also believe (Mark 1:15). In another passage Paul mentions the twofold necessity of repentance and faith as conditions for salvation (see Acts 20:21). Paul's response to the Philippian jailer's question was: "Believe on the Lord Jesus Christ, and thou shalt be saved" (16:31).

To believe means to accept what God's Word says about the Lord Jesus Christ. Christ died for our sins (1 Corinthians 15:3). He shed His precious blood that by it we might be cleansed from them (Ephesians 1:7; 1 John 1:7).

We must also believe in the resurrection of the Lord Jesus Christ from the dead (Romans 10:9). By raising Jesus from the dead, God demonstrated His approval upon the redemptive work of His Son on the cross. Just as God gave new life to the lifeless body of Jesus, so He gives spiritual and eternal life to those who believe in Jesus as Lord and Saviour (Ephesians 2:1).

3. *Confession.* After repenting of our sins and believing in Jesus as Saviour and Lord, we are required to confess Him openly. This condition is given also in Romans 10:9,10 which says: "If thou shalt confess with thy mouth the Lord Jesus, . . . thou shalt be saved. For with the heart man believeth unto righteousness; and with the mouth confession is made unto salvation." A saved person is not ashamed of his Lord.

47

Do Good Works Save Us?

Do you remember Jesus' story about the Pharisee and the publican (Luke 18:10-14)? Many people are like the Pharisee. He depended on his good works, such as fasting and paying tithes, to give him acceptance in God's sight. The publican (a despised tax collector), on the other hand, simply called upon God to be merciful to him, recognizing he was a sinner in God's sight.

The teaching that salvation is based on good works is called *legalism.* The legalistic approach says that one must observe God's laws to be saved.

The Roman Catholic Church. This church teaches that faith alone is not enough for salvation. It must be accompanied by works. In other words, we obtain salvation by faith plus works. This is one of the major differences between Roman Catholic teaching and evangelical Protestant teaching. In effect, Roman Catholicism teaches that the work of Jesus Christ on the cross was not enough; we must add something to it—our good works.

Seventh-Day Adventism. In many respects this denomination is very orthodox in its teaching. Adventists, like our Roman Catholic friends, believe in the deity of the Lord Jesus Christ, His virgin birth, His atoning death, and His bodily resurrection. They also teach that forgiveness of sins comes by God's grace.

But they have a mixture of faith and works in their understanding of salvation. They insist that the special day of worship must be the "Sabbath" or Saturday. To observe any other day as the Lord's Day, such as Sunday, is wrong. Mrs. Ellen White, one of the early leaders of the Seventh-Day Adventist Church, went so far as to say that Sunday observance is the mark of the beast referred to in Revelation 16:2 (*The Great Controversy Between Christ and*

Satan [Mountain View: Pacific Press, 1911 ed.], p. 449).

Mormonism. This cult teaches the necessity of works for salvation. Even though Christ died for the sins of the world, the sinner cannot be justified by faith alone. According to Mormonism's teaching, the death of Christ removed the penalty of sin, but man is still required to perform good works to be saved. Being saved, according to this group, means that eventually a person will become a god. It seems that they prefer to use the term *exaltation* rather than *salvation*.

Christian Science. This group also distorts the Biblical view of salvation. In the official guidebook of the denomination we read the following: "One sacrifice however great is insufficient to pay the debt of sin. The atonement requires constant self-immolation on the sinner's part" (*Science and Health,* p. 23).

As we saw in the preceding chapter, Christian Science teaches that sin is unreal and that this erroneous idea of sin as a reality must be overcome. In other words, salvation does not come by accepting the death of Jesus on the cross and the cleansing of His blood, but by casting out the idea of sin.

Unitarianism and Liberal Protestant Churches. These teach that Jesus was a good man, but that He was not God. They reject the idea that He died as a substitute for others. Their teaching is that we save ourselves by following His good example.

Jehovah's Witnesses. This cult places much emphasis on observing the Law in order to be saved. They teach that the death of Christ canceled Adam's sin and its consequence, death. They also teach that because the consequences of sin were canceled by Christ, we have a chance to earn merit by our good works.

What the Bible Teaches

From beginning to end the Bible emphasizes that we cannot be saved by our good works or a combination of faith and good works. The Book of Galatians is especially directed against this erroneous teaching that says good works are necessary for a person to be saved.

The apostle Paul says: "Knowing that a man is not justified by the works of the law, but by the faith of Jesus Christ, even we have believed in Jesus Christ, that we might be justified by the faith of Christ, and not by the works of the law: for by the works of the law shall no flesh be justified" (Galatians 2:16).

He says further that if anything is added to this requirement of faith in Christ, then Jesus died for nothing. "I do not frustrate the grace of God: for if righteousness come by the law, then Christ is dead in vain" (v. 21). If we make even a single work a requirement for salvation in addition to faith, this cancels out the faith.

"I testify again to every man that is circumcised, that he is a debtor to do the whole law. Christ is become of no effect unto you, whosoever of you are justified by the law; ye are fallen from grace" (5:3,4). The emphasis throughout this book is that faith, not faith plus works, is the condition for salvation.

Perhaps you are asking at this point: "But what is the place of works in salvation?" We know, of course, that it is "not by works of righteousness which we have done, but according to his mercy he saved us" (Titus 3:5). We also know that salvation is "not of works, lest any man should boast" (Ephesians 2:9). But we read in the next verse that even though we are saved by grace through faith, we have been "created in Christ Jesus unto good works" (v. 10).

Paul tells us in another place to "work out your own salvation with fear and trembling" (Philippians 2:12). But we must notice that we are not to work *for* our salvation but to work *out* the salvation we already have. When a person has truly repented and believed in Christ as His Saviour, he is a new creature in Christ (2 Corinthians 5:17). Good works then will be the *effect* of salvation, not its cause. This is what James meant when he said: "I will show thee my faith by my works" (James 2:18). In other words, a truly saved person will lead a changed life.

We have all read stories of drowning people being saved. A drowning person often struggles so hard that he only endangers himself further. To be saved he must place himself completely in the hands of his rescuer. He must stop struggling. This is how it is with God. As long as we depend on our own efforts, He cannot save us. When we place ourselves completely in His hands, He does what we were unable to do for ourselves.

Water Baptism

Students often ask me, "Is it necessary to be baptized in water?" My response usually is, "Necessary for what?" Baptism is not necessary for salvation.

Erroneous teachings about baptism. The teaching that baptism is necessary for salvation is called baptismal regeneration. It says that a person's sins are washed away by the act of baptism.

The Roman Catholic and Lutheran churches teach very strongly that baptism washes away sins. This teaching is based on a belief that infants come into the world as sinners and that the rite of baptism is necessary for them to be cleansed of the sin inherited from Adam. According to this teaching, baptism washes away this "original sin."

51

Mormons also believe baptism is necessary for salvation. They even practice proxy baptism. A living Mormon may be baptized on behalf of a dead person who, they believe, will have the "gospel" preached to him in the spirit world.

The Church of Christ teaches that baptism is the final requirement a person must meet if he wants his sins forgiven. They do stress the need of repentance and a changed life, but baptism is also necessary to meet all the requirements.

What the Bible Says

You must understand that water baptism is very important in the teaching of the New Testament. Jesus commanded the disciples to baptize people (Matthew 28:19). But the doctrine of baptismal regeneration confuses what is necessary for salvation with what God requires *after* a person is saved.

The repentant thief on the cross certainly was not baptized. Yet Jesus said to him: "Today shalt thou be with me in paradise" (Luke 23:43). Cornelius and his household were saved and filled with the Holy Spirit; but they had not yet been baptized in water (Acts 10:44-48).

Water baptism is important to the Christian. It is a testimony to others about what the Lord has done for him. By the act of immersion we testify that we have identified ourselves with the death and resurrection of Jesus and that we are new creatures in Him (Romans 6:3-6).

The close connection between salvation and baptism as a picture of salvation is shown in Jesus' words: "He that believeth and is baptized shall be saved" (Mark 16:16). But notice that neither Jesus nor anyone else in the New Testament ever said something like, "He that is not baptized shall be damned." Baptism should normally follow repentance and faith as soon as possible, as a believer's first act of obedience to his Lord, but it is not necessary for salvation.

The Mormon practice of baptism for the dead misinterprets 1 Corinthians 15:29. In that passage Paul is simply referring to the practice of some people without approving it. He is making the point that even those who baptize for the dead (erroneously) have a belief in the resurrection of the body. How much more should Christians have such a belief in the Resurrection? Furthermore, nowhere does the Bible teach that one person can do anything to contribute to another person's salvation. Salvation is personal.

The practice of infant baptism likewise has no basis in the New Testament. This practice seems to have developed in the second century.

Another erroneous view of baptism is held by the "Oneness" or "Jesus Only" people who were mentioned in the preceding chapter. Their teaching is that baptism must be in the name of Jesus only. Behind this belief is a denial of the doctrine of the Trinity. According to these people, the only valid baptism is in Jesus' name. But Jesus himself told the disciples to baptize "in the name of the Father, and of the Son, and of the Holy Ghost" (Matthew 28:19).

When the Book of Acts talks about baptism in the name of Jesus or in the name of the Lord (2:38; 8:16; 10:48; 19:5), this is to distinguish it from the baptism of John. Even some pagan religions of the first century had baptismal ceremonies. The disciples in the Book of Acts were stressing that their hearers must submit to Christian baptism which would be a symbol of their death and resurrection with Christ (Romans 6:3-6).

The Baptism in the Holy Spirit

Some Pentecostals teach that the baptism in the Holy Spirit is necessary for salvation. This error is often based on a misinterpretation of the Parable of the Ten Virgins (Matthew 25:1-13). The teaching of the parable, according to these people, is that the virgins without oil were those who had not been baptized in the Holy Spirit and consequently were not prepared to meet the Lord.

It is certainly true that oil in the Bible often symbolizes the Holy Spirit. But it is not necessary to take this to mean the baptism in the Holy Spirit. If the oil in the parable does indeed speak of the Holy Spirit, then it is talking about the work of the Holy Spirit in regeneration (John 3:5), rather than the baptism in the Holy Spirit. "If any man have not the Spirit of Christ, he is none of his" (Romans 8:9).

6

What Is the Church?

My first position as a Bible college teacher was in Lakeland, Florida. Shortly after we arrived there, a faculty couple with whom we had become acquainted came to our house. It was in the evening, and Ken said to me, "Let's run over to McDonald's for hamburgers." I tried not to display my shock at what he had said. I replied something like, "Not this evening."

Some days later I discovered what he meant, and realized I had misinterpreted him. Ken was talking about the hamburger chain called McDonald's. I did not know of any such eating places. We did not have them in New Jersey where I had been living. The only "McDonald's" I knew was a faculty couple named MacDonald who lived next door to us, and I thought Ken was saying, "Let's go next door and have Mrs. MacDonald make hamburgers for us."

Sometimes it is that way with the words we use in discussing matters pertaining to the Bible. The word *church* means different things to different people. In this chapter you will see what the Bible means when it uses this word.

The New Testament Use of the Word

The word *church* in our New Testament comes from the Greek *ekklesia*. It was a common word in the first century among Greek-speaking people. It designated the group of men who left their homes or places of business to conduct the business of the community. Sometimes it was used simply for a gathering of people (see Acts 19:32,39,41).

This Greek word is made up of two parts. The first part (*ek*) means "out of" and the second part (*klesia*) comes from a word meaning "to call." The original meaning of the word therefore is "to call out of." Greek scholars generally agree that the best translation for this word is *assembly* rather than *church*. When it is used in the Bible for God's people, it suggests that they have been "called out of" sin and the world and have come together to worship and serve Him.

The word is used in the New Testament in two ways:

1. *The universal Church.* The universal Church is sometimes called the invisible Church. It consists of all who have been born again regardless of location or time. When the word is used this way, it is always in the singular—the Church (Ephesians 1:22; 3:21; Hebrews 12:23). It emphasizes that all who have been washed in the blood of Jesus, wherever they are, are one in Him.

The universal Church is such a wonderful organism that it is impossible to describe it fully. But the apostle Paul and other New Testament writers, directed by the Holy Spirit, use figures of speech that help us understand more fully the nature of the Church:

a. Sometimes they speak of the Church as the bride of Christ (2 Corinthians 11:2; Ephesians 5:25,27; Revelation 19:7; 22:17). This emphasizes the purity of the Church, which has been cleansed by the blood of Jesus. He is the Bridegroom (Matthew 25:6;

John 3:29). When He returns, the Bride will be married to her heavenly Groom (Revelation 19:7-9; 21:2).

b. We can think of the Church as a building, and especially as a temple (1 Corinthians 3:9,16,17; 2 Corinthians 6:16; Ephesians 2:20-22; 1 Timothy 3:15; 1 Peter 2:5; Revelation 21:3). The tabernacle and the temple in the Old Testament were places where God manifested His presence in a special way. But God does not really dwell in physical buildings (Acts 7:48,49; 17:24,25).

Today His special presence is manifested in and through the Church, which is His spiritual temple. Jesus Christ is the chief Cornerstone of this Temple, the apostles and prophets are its foundation (Ephesians 2:20-22), and each believer is a "living stone" (1 Peter 2:5).

c. The universal Church is also likened to a human body (Romans 12:4,5; 1 Corinthians 12:22-27; Ephesians 1:22,23; 3:6). When you study these passages, you will notice the following important points:

(1) Jesus Christ is the Head of the Church.
(2) Every born-again person belongs to this Body.
(3) Every member is related directly to the Head, the Lord Jesus Christ. He is the "nerve center" of the Body.
(4) Individual members of the Body must recognize their dependence on one another.
(5) Every member of this Body is supposed to support and strengthen the others.
(6) Every member has a vital function in the Body, even though it may seem insignificant.
(7) Today the Lord Jesus Christ manifests himself to the world through His spiritual body, the Church, just as when He was on earth He manifested himself through His physical body.

The universal Church is a spiritual organism that includes all who have been born again. A spiritual, invisible bond unites all true believers. Therefore, it is often referred to as the "invisible" Church because God alone can determine who belongs to it.

2. *The local church.* The New Testament also uses the word *ekklesia* to designate a local congregation of Christians. The universal, invisible Church can never meet as a group on earth. But it manifests itself in local groups of believers.

In New Testament times these local groups often met in houses (see Romans 16:5; Colossians 4:15). Sometimes they were identified with a city. Paul wrote to "the church of God which is at Corinth" (1 Corinthians 1:2) and to "the church of the Thessalonians " (1 Thessalonians 1:1; 2 Thessalonians 1:1). The plural is sometimes used, such as when he wrote to "the churches of Galatia" (Galatians 1:2).

You must distinguish between the invisible Church and the visible church. The visible church meets in local congregations. But, unfortunately, not everyone who belongs to a local congregation is a member of the invisible, universal Church. Some denominations admit members who are not truly saved. Sometimes, a person may appear to be a Christian without having a genuine conversion experience. And that person may be accepted into membership.

Therefore, we must be careful not to think that the invisible Church consists of all members of the visible church. The Parable of the Tares and the Wheat makes this clear (Matthew 13:24-30,36-43). Sometimes tares are indistinguishable from wheat.

The Purpose of the Church

The overall purpose of the Church is that it should

be to the praise of God's glory (Ephesians 1:6,12,14). The way the Church glorifies God is three-directional: outwardly, by evangelizing the world; inwardly, by believers edifying one another; and upwardly, by worshiping God.

1. *Evangelization.* The word *evangelism* literally means "a declaration or preaching of the gospel." The world is the field for evangelization, as Jesus commanded (Matthew 28:19,20; Mark 16:15). We must share the gospel with all men everywhere. Jesus told His disciples they were to be witnesses both near home (Jerusalem, Judea, Samaria) and in distant lands (the uttermost parts of the earth), as we see in Acts 1:8. The Book of Acts gives a wonderful account of how the Early Church followed His command.

2. *Edification.* The Church as the body of Christ must be healthy. Individual members must edify or build up one another. This is one of the purposes of gathering for worship (1 Corinthians 14:26). Christians are to teach and admonish one another (Ephesians 5:18,19; Colossians 3:16) and to help a sinning brother (Galatians 6:1,2; James 5:19,20). We must also pray for one another (Ephesians 1:16-22).

3. *Worship.* The Church is God's temple, and individual members are priests who offer themselves and their praises as sacrifices to God (Romans 12:1; Hebrews 13:15). When we come together to "minister to the Lord," the Holy Spirit will be able to speak to us (Acts 13:2,3). This worship must be in spirit and in truth (John 4:23,24). Under the direction of the Holy Spirit, we seek to glorify God by means of song, praise, prayer, and the ministry of His Word. A Spirit-filled congregation also experiences spiritual gifts in its worship (1 Corinthians 14).

Non-Biblical Meanings of the Word *Church*

Two modern uses of the word *church* are not found in Scripture. Sometimes a denomination is referred to as a church—such as the Episcopal Church, the United Methodist Church, the American Lutheran Church. Also, a building in which Christians worship is often called a church. Since these two usages are so common, and it is impractical to try to change the dictionary, we must be clear in our understanding of what the New Testament means by the word. And we must also be sure when we use the word that others understand what we mean by it.

The Roman Catholic Church

When Roman Catholics say "the Church" they do not mean all believers everywhere. They mean the organization that has its headquarters in Rome and is called the Roman Catholic Church.

The Apostles' Creed (which probably originated in the second century and was not really composed by the apostles) is recited in many churches during a Sunday morning service. The Roman Catholic Church emphasizes that the Apostles' Creed says: "I believe in . . . the holy Catholic Church." But the word *catholic* is simply an old word meaning "universal." As we have already seen, every believer is a member of the universal or catholic Church because he is a part of the body of Christ. It is presumptuous for any denomination to say it is the universal Church.

The Roman Catholic Church claims to be the one true Church because of its belief that Peter was the first pastor or bishop of the congregation in Rome, and therefore was the first pope. It teaches that Jesus gave supreme authority in the Church to Peter, and that the popes are Peter's successors.

It bases much of its belief on Jesus' words to Peter: "I say also unto thee, That thou art Peter, and upon this rock I will build my church; and the gates of hell shall not prevail against it. And I will give unto thee the keys of the kingdom of heaven: and whatsoever thou shalt bind on earth shall be bound in heaven; and whatsoever thou shalt loose on earth shall be loosed in heaven" (Matthew 16:18,19).

We need to understand correctly what Jesus actually meant. The name *Peter* means rock or stone, but is this the rock on which Jesus has built His church? Notice Jesus did not say, "You are Peter and upon you I will build my Church." Peter would be a very shaky foundation. Immediately after this incident, Jesus told the disciples how He must suffer and die. Then we are told Peter rebuked Him for saying this. Jesus responded: "Get thee behind me, Satan" (Matthew 16:23).

The Lord Jesus Christ is the Rock upon which the Church is built. Paul says: "For other foundation can no man lay than that is laid, which is Jesus Christ" (1 Corinthians 3:11). He is the Rock, the chief Cornerstone (see Ephesians 2:20). We may look at it another way by saying that the foundation of the Church is the confession of faith made by Peter: "Thou art the Christ, the Son of the living God" (Matthew 16:16).

What did Jesus mean when He told Peter He would give him the keys of the kingdom of heaven? We know that Peter was the instrument God used to open the doors of the kingdom of heaven to both the Jews (Acts 2) and the Gentiles (Acts 10). We also know that Peter was the leader of the Early Church in Jerusalem (Acts 1:15; Galatians 1:18). But there is not one shred of evidence in the New Testament that Peter was ever in Rome, much less that he was the pastor or bishop of the congregation in Rome.

Is the Church a Spiritually Elite Group?

Many sects identify the Church with a small group of persons who are supposed to belong to a spiritually elite group. This is an error that characterizes most cults, and sometimes is even found in the Pentecostal Movement. Some believe that only those who have been baptized in the Holy Spirit or are "overcomers" constitute the true Church.

Jehovah's Witnesses are one of the main offenders. They make a distinction between those who inherit the heavenly kingdom and those who will reign on earth. Here is a quotation from one of their official publications: "Those following Him (Christ) who become His spiritual brothers and joint heirs in the Kingdom are comparatively few, just 144,000 in number, and so He calls them a 'little flock' (Luke 12:33)."

They claim that only this number will enter into "the Kingdom sheepfold." Others who believe in Jesus and follow Him as Shepherd "become members of His flock, though not of the Kingdom fold. They attain to eternal life on earth" (*This Means Everlasting Life* [Brooklyn: Watchtower Bible Tract Society, 1950], pp. 237, 238).

In connection with this, Jehovah's Witnesses have a peculiar understanding of the Lord's Supper. They celebrate it once a year on the evening of the Jewish Passover. Only those who know they belong to the 144,000 are allowed to partake.

The New Testament never makes any distinction between believers who constitute the Church and believers who belong to some other group. All believers constitute the Church. "For by one Spirit are we all baptized into one body, whether we be Jews or Gentiles, whether we be bond or free; and have been all made to drink into one Spirit" (1 Corinthians 12:13). Every believer is a member of the Church, the body of Christ. Even the apostle Paul did not put himself in a special class (see Philippians 3:12-14). There are no second-rate Christians in the Church!

All Mankind Belongs to the Church

Many people who are liberal in their theology say that because God is the Father of all mankind all men are brothers. They are saying in another way that all men eventually will be saved; therefore, all men belong to the Church. Sometimes they express it in language such as: "Every man has a spark of divinity in him," or, "The Christ is in all of us." This view is just the opposite of the preceding one of the Church being a spiritually elite group.

Sometimes the teaching of the New Testament is twisted by these people. They argue that because the Bible teaches that Christ died for all, therefore all men are saved—if not now, then eventually. But the Bible clearly places conditions upon being saved, as we saw in chapter 3. It is only when people meet those conditions that they are added to the Church. "And the Lord was adding to their number day by day those who were being saved" (Acts 2:47, *NASB*).

7

Do We Need Mediators?

Countries are a lot like people. Sometimes two countries will not be on speaking terms. This has been the situation for many years between Israel and her Arab neighbors. Both sides realize something must be done to settle the dispute.

To "save face" and make it easier for all concerned, in situations like this a third party carries on communication between the two opposing parties. In recent years the United States secretary of state has performed this function.

A mediator is a go-between. He represents each side to the other. In the realm of the spiritual and our relationship with God, what does the Bible have to say about mediators?

Only One Mediator

The Lord Jesus Christ is the only Mediator between God and men (1 Timothy 2:5). He himself said: "I am the way, the truth, and the life: no man cometh unto the Father, but by me" (John 14:6). Jesus Christ is the only valid Mediator between us and God because He is both man and God. It is difficult for our finite minds to understand how one Being can be both, but this is the teaching of Scripture and we accept it.

The New Testament also expresses this idea of

Jesus as the Mediator by calling Him our High Priest (Hebrews 4:14-16). This wonderful High Priest "ever liveth to make intercession" for us (7:25). Because of our sins, we cannot go directly to God. But because Jesus Christ, the High Priest, made atonement for our sins we may go to the Father through Him.

Another way of stating this idea of the mediation of Jesus is in the words of the apostle John when he says: "If any man sin, we have an advocate with the Father, Jesus Christ the righteous" (1 John 2:1). Jesus is like a lawyer pleading our case before the Judge of the universe. He stands between us and the judgment of God.

Who Can Forgive Sins?

The Roman Catholic Church teaches that God forgives sins through its priests. According to this teaching, a priest is God's representative on earth who can refuse or grant forgiveness of sins. This teaching says that Jesus promised this authority to the Roman Catholic Church when He said to Peter: "Whatsoever thou shalt bind on earth shall be bound in heaven; and whatsoever thou shalt loose on earth shall be loosed in heaven" (Matthew 16:19). This power, it is claimed, was then extended to all the apostles (18:18). They further quote Jesus' words in John 20:23: "Whosoever sins ye remit, they are remitted unto them; and whosoever sins ye retain, they are retained."

A Roman Catholic receives forgiveness by "going to confession." The person confesses his sins to the priest and indicates sorrow for them. Then the priest, in the name of the Church, pronounces absolution or forgiveness if he thinks the person is truly repentant. This procedure is called "auricular confession," which means "confession in the ear" of the priest.

Nowhere in the Bible do we find any record of anyone ever going to a leader in the Church and enumerating his sins to that leader to receive forgiveness. This practice was a later development in the history of the Church. Confession to God is all that is necessary. "If we confess our sins, he is faithful and just to forgive us our sins, and to cleanse us from all unrighteousness" (1 John 1:9). Jesus himself said: "Who can forgive sins but God only?" (Mark 2:7).

We do find in the New Testament, however, that sometimes it is helpful to acknowledge sins to fellow Christians. "Confess your sins to one another, and pray for one another, so that you may be healed" (James 5:16, NASB). But notice that this is talking about acknowledging our sins to one another and not to a leader in the Church. Furthermore, nothing is said about anyone forgiving us of our sins in the sense that such a person can remove our sins from us.

We must come back to what Jesus meant when He seemed to confer on His followers the authority to forgive sins. Since the Bible is so clear that man cannot forgive sins, those words of Jesus must be understood in that light. In the previous chapter we discussed how Jesus gave Peter the keys of the Kingdom, which meant that God used Peter to open the door of salvation to both Jews and Gentiles.

When we are faithful in proclaiming the gospel, we are instrumental in God's hands in offering forgiveness of sins. When sinners hear the gospel from us and repent, their sins are forgiven as a result of our faithfulness. Indirectly, we are forgiving their sins. Likewise, when they refuse to respond to the gospel, their sins are not forgiven, and indirectly we retain their sins.

The apostle Paul tells us that God has given to us

"the ministry of reconciliation" (2 Corinthians 5:18). He goes on to say: "Now then we are ambassadors for Christ, as though God did beseech you by us: we pray you in Christ's stead, be ye reconciled to God" (v. 20). The Lord has given to His church the authority to confirm that an individual is saved if he has repented of his sins and received Christ as his Lord and Saviour.

The Idea of the "Mass"

The Roman Catholic Church teaches that only a priest is authorized to offer "Mass." It says that the Mass is the central act of worship. The word *Mass* comes from the Latin term *missum,* which means "dismissal." In earlier centuries in the Roman Catholic Church, persons attending the service who were not Christians were dismissed before the Lord's Supper was observed. The priest would say, "Missa est," which means, "You are dismissed." The Lord's Supper was considered to be so sacred that only Christians were allowed to be present.

The official teaching of the Roman Catholic Church is that at the time of the celebration of the Eucharist (a term used often for the Lord's Supper) the priest transforms the bread and wine into the actual physical body and blood of Christ. This change which they say takes place is called "transubstantiation."

The Roman Catholic Church also teaches that at the celebration of the Mass the sacrifice of Christ takes place all over again. Sometimes this is called "the unbloody sacrifice of the Cross." But this idea of a repeated sacrifice completely contradicts the teaching of the New Testament. In Hebrews 9:26 we read that "now once in the end of the world hath he appeared to put away sin by the sacrifice of himself." In verse 28 we read: "Christ was once offered to bear the sins of many." In the next chapter we are told that Christ, "after he had offered one sacrifice for sins for ever, sat down on the right hand of God" (10:12; see also v. 14).

In its idea of the priesthood, the Roman Catholic Church continues the idea of the Old Testament priesthood. It does not recognize the fact that all that the Old Testament priests did was fulfilled in Christ because He is the great High Priest. Not only is He the High Priest, He is also God's eternal sacrifice for our sins (John 1:29). His death on the cross was the once-for-all sacrifice for sin, so that we have no need of priests today to offer any other sacrifices.

What does the New Testament say about the teaching that the communion bread and wine actually become the body and blood of Christ? Roman Catholics have completely misunderstood Jesus' words, "This is my body," and, "This is my blood" (Mark 14:22,24). At the time Jesus made those statements He was physically present with His disciples in the Upper Room. How could He mean that the bread and wine were actually His body when His actual body was offering them the bread and wine?

The Roman Catholic doctrine of transubstantiation has no basis in the New Testament. The simple and correct understanding of the words of Jesus is that they are figures of speech called "metaphors." The dictionary definition of a metaphor is that it is "a figure of speech in which one thing is likened to another different thing by being spoken of as if it were that other; implied comparison in which a word or phrase ordinarily and primarily used of one thing is applied to another." We all use metaphors in everyday speech. Haven't you heard expressions like, "She's a jewel," or, "He's a tiger"?

In other words, Jesus was saying, "This bread represents my body," and, "This wine represents my blood." When we partake of the Lord's Supper, we are reminded by those two symbols of the death of Jesus for us.

Praying to the Saints

The Roman Catholic Church teaches that its followers ought to pray to the saints. In Roman Catholic teaching, a saint is a person who lived a very godly life and whom the Church recognizes as having been responsible for performing some miracles. The teaching goes on to say that because these people lived such God-fearing lives, they now have special access to God's presence. Therefore, we ought to pray to them. We should also honor them.

Even though many Roman Catholics virtually worship the saints, the official teaching of the Roman Catholic Church is that the saints are to be venerated, not worshiped. God alone is to be worshiped. It uses three words, coming from the Latin language, to make this kind of distinction. It says that *latria* is the worship due only to God. *Dulia* is the honor and veneration given to the saints. But Mary, the mother of Jesus, is in a special category. She is not God, but she is to be the most honored of all saints. Therefore, the veneration given to her is called *hyperdulia*.

Again, this teaching of the Roman Catholic Church has no foundation at all in Scripture. Nowhere in the Bible do we find anyone praying to a deceased godly person. Jesus Christ is still the only Mediator between God and men. Yet one of the most frequently uttered prayers in the Roman Catholic Church is addressed to Mary. The latter half of that prayer, which is called "The Hail Mary," says: "Holy Mary, Mother of God, pray for us sinners now and at the hour of our death."

The veneration of Mary is so extensive and deep-rooted that many Roman Catholic theologians also refer to her as the co-mediatrix or co-redemptrix. In other words, they place her alongside Christ in His roles as Mediator and Redeemer.

Bible-believing Christians must of course recognize that Mary and many other "saints" were very godly people who served their Lord faithfully. Yet we must also remember that they were mortal beings like us. When they died, they went to be with the Lord. If, as Roman Catholics believe, anyone anywhere on the face of the earth can pray to these saints, then it means that the saints are omnipresent (that is, that they are present everywhere at the same time). This is clearly contrary to Scripture, which teaches that only God is omnipresent.

We must also see that when the word *saints* is used in the Bible, it refers to *living* Christians. As a matter of fact, all Christians are called saints (Romans 1:7; 2 Corinthians 1:1; Ephesians 1:1). The word *saint* comes from a Greek word meaning "separated one." It is not talking about the advanced spiritual state of any person. It simply calls attention to the fact that Christians have been called from the world and a life of sin and are now living their lives in relation to God.

The Priesthood of All Believers

Contrary to the teaching of the Roman Catholic Church, the New Testament teaches that all believers are spiritual priests (1 Peter 2:5,9; Revelation 1:6). This means we all have direct access to God's presence. It is not necessary for us to have a mediator, either alive or dead, for God to hear us. Martin

Luther and the other Protestant reformers were very strong on this point because they were convinced of the teaching of the Scriptures. This doctrine is called the "universal priesthood of believers."

We saw in the previous chapter that the Church is God's spiritual temple. We are the spiritual priests. As priests, we too offer sacrifices to God. The New Testament mentions at least three such sacrifices.

We offer our bodies as living sacrifices to the Lord. This is called our "spiritual service of worship" (Romans 12:1, NASB). We also offer our praises to God. In the Jewish temple animal sacrifices were made daily, so there was a continual burning of their bodies. The smoke and the aroma that ascended to God was pleasing in His sight when the sacrifices were offered with a repentant heart. With this in mind, Christians are told to "offer the sacrifice of praise to God continually, that is, the fruit of our lips, giving thanks to his name" (Hebrews 13:15). We are also told: Do not neglect doing good and sharing; for with such sacrifices God is pleased" (v. 16, NASB).

Pastors, Not Priests

Even though all believers are spiritual priests, God has appointed leaders in the Church. In a local congregation the leader is called a *pastor*. The Greek word for pastor is the same as the word for shepherd (*poimen*). From this we see that the pastor is responsible for the spiritual needs of his flock—the congregation (Ephesians 4:11; John 21:15-17; Acts 20:28).

Pastors are also called elders and bishops. All three terms are used interchangeably in the New Testament (see Acts 20:17-28). By calling them elders, the emphasis is on their spiritual maturity. When they are called bishops, it indicates that they have oversight of God's work (the Greek word for bishop actually means "overseer"). The qualifications for these leaders are given in 1 Timothy 3:2-7 and Titus 1:7-9.

3 Characteristics of Personality

(2) ROM 15:30   EPH 4:30
    ISA 63:10

(3) I COR 12:11

II Personal Pronouns
    JOHN 14: 16,17, 15: 26
    JOHN 16: 7,8

III PERSONAL ACTS

MK 13:11   LK 2:26
ACTS 13:2   ACTS 5:32
ACTS 21:11   ROM 8:16
I TIM 4:1   I COR 2:10
REV 2:7   ROM 8:26
JOHN 14:16

Holy Spirit speaks, reveals,
witnesses, searches, prays, intercedes
teaches, guides

What Is the Holy Spirit's Work?

The Christian Church has always believed in the Holy Spirit. But in the 20th century, more than at any other time in the Church's history, Christians are studying about and experiencing the work of the Holy Spirit.

Many years ago a noted theologian wrote an article titled "The Cinderella of Theology." In it he stressed how the Church had always given much attention to the Father and the Son, but not the Holy Spirit. All this has changed. At the turn of the 20th century, God poured out the Holy Spirit in a marvelous way. The modern Pentecostal Movement and charismatic movement are the results of this. Because of this renewed interest in the Holy Spirit, you will want to know more about this third Person of the Trinity.

The Holy Spirit Is a Person

Many people, even some Bible-believing Christians, do not think of the Holy Spirit as a Person. Yet when we examine the Scriptures, we discover that it says many things about the Spirit to indicate that He is indeed a Person. Part of our problem is that we have difficulty understanding how a spirit can be a person. But it is not necessary for a person to have a body. God the Father is a Person, yet He does not have a body. Let us look at some of the scriptural evidence that shows the personality of the Holy Spirit.

The Holy Spirit has a mind, a will, and emotions. These are essential parts in the makeup of a person. We read about "the mind of the Spirit" (Romans 8:27). We read also that the Spirit distributes spiritual gifts "to each one individually just as He wills" (1 Corinthians 12:11, *NASB*). He also may be grieved or vexed, showing that He has emotions (Ephesians 4:30; Isaiah 63:10).

We see also that many of the works of the Holy Spirit can be performed only by persons. The Holy Spirit took part in Creation (Genesis 1:2). He convicts or convinces men of their sin (John 16:8). He also intercedes for us (Romans 8:26). He speaks, He teaches, and He testifies (John 16:13; 14:26; 15:26).

The personality of the Holy Spirit is denied by some of the major cults. Jehovah's Witnesses say simply that the Holy Spirit "is the invisible force of the almighty God that moved His servants to do His will" (*Let God Be True*, [Brooklyn: Watchtower Bible and Tract Society, 1952], pp. 81, 89). They also deny that the Holy Spirit is a member of the Godhead.

The Mormons teach that there are many gods, as we saw in chapter 2. The only difference they see between the Holy Spirit and other gods is that the Holy Spirit is less material (Joseph Smith, *Compendium of Doctrine*, p. 259). By saying that the Holy Spirit is material, Mormonism actually denies the essential nature of the Holy Spirit—that a spirit just cannot be material. Spirits can only *manifest* themselves in physical form.

Christian Science likewise denies the deity and personality of the Holy Spirit. Mary Baker Eddy, its founder, wrote: "In the words of St. John: 'He shall give you another Comforter, that He may abide with you forever' this Comforter I understand to be Divine Science" (*Science and Health,* p. 55).

It is not always easy to understand the doctrine of the Holy Spirit, but we do know the Scriptures clearly teach that He is a Person and that He is a member of the Holy Trinity. The work of the Holy Spirit is very extensive. In chapter 4 we already talked about the work of the Holy Spirit in convicting of sin and regenerating a person who repents and believes. In the remainder of this chapter we will consider two of His other works.

We will now talk about the work of the Holy Spirit in sanctification and in the baptism in the Holy Spirit.

✳ Sanctification

Sanctification is one of the most controversial subjects in the history of Protestantism and the Pentecostal Movement. One writer has said it is tempting "to wonder how many persons have evidenced lack of sanctification in heated argument over the doctrine of sanctification."

The two Greek words for sanctification occur a total of 13 times in the New Testament. About half of these times the translation is "holiness." Now we know why it is such an important doctrine; the doctrine of sanctification is the doctrine of holiness.

Sanctification is God's will for us (1 Thessalonians 4:3), without which we cannot see God (Hebrews 12:14). It is a special work of the Holy Spirit (2 Thessalonians 2:13; 1 Peter 1:2).

Erroneous Views of Sanctification

The basic meaning of the Greek words for sanctification is separation. When Christians are told to be holy, God is asking them to separate themselves from

75

sin and to dedicate themselves to Him. The words *dedication* and *consecration* can sometimes be used to translate these Greek words. Misunderstandings related to this idea of sanctification result from lack of understanding of the Biblical doctrine. These misunderstandings are:

1. *Legalism.* This is the view that a person is sanctified only if he lives in complete obedience to the law of God. Sanctification consists of following prescribed regulations. This viewpoint teaches that our salvation and the retaining of our salvation depends on our good works rather than faith. Many times those who hold this view have a long list of dos and don'ts.

The apostle Paul dealt with this problem when he wrote to the Galatian Christians. He asked them: "Are you so foolish? having begun in the Spirit, are ye now made perfect by the flesh?" (Galatians 3:3). The legalistic approach does not seem to understand what the Word of God teaches—that a person who depends on the Law is obligated to obey it in every detail; otherwise, God's curse will be upon him (Deuteronomy 27:26).

According to the Scriptures, our Christian life is by faith, not works. True faith will produce genuine Christian works, which we call the fruit of the Spirit (Ephesians 2:8-10; Galatians 5:22,23). But it is wrong to teach that good works in themselves guarantee salvation and sanctification.

2. *Libertinism.* This is the opposite of legalism. It teaches that it makes no difference how a person lives. It says that a Christian has been freed by Christ; therefore, he may do what he pleases. But Paul argues against this position by saying: "Use not liberty for an occasion to the flesh, but by love serve one another" (v. 13). We must say again that a per-

son who has been truly born again by the Spirit of God will demonstrate love toward God and others.

3. *A second definite work of grace.* This is the teaching of the Holiness Movement. It says that sanctification is something completely distinct from the conversion experience. In the first crisis experience of salvation, we receive forgiveness of sin. But in the second crisis experience of sanctification, we receive victory over sin. Some Pentecostal groups, like the Pentecostal Holiness Church and the Church of God (Cleveland, Tennessee), hold this view of sanctification. But within the Holiness Movement there is no uniform belief as to the extent or degree of this victory over sin.

Erroneous One form of this view says that sanctification consists of the eradication of man's sinful nature. A "sanctified" Christian is one whose sinful nature has been completely eradicated so he is unable to sin. Another viewpoint says that the experience gives a person the ability not to sin.

The Bible teaches that we are sanctified by the blood of Jesus (Hebrews 10:10; 13:12). This happens at the time we believe in Jesus as our Saviour. Sanctification is sometimes spoken of as a past experience (1 Corinthians 6:11). It happened when we were saved (1:30).

But the Bible also teaches what we may call "progressive sanctification." We must not be satisfied with any degree of spiritual progress or level of maturity we have obtained. Paul himself was constantly pressing on toward a goal (Philippians 3:10-14). We must "cleanse ourselves from all filthiness of the flesh and spirit, perfecting holiness in the fear of God" (2 Corinthians 7:1).

How can we experience this progressive sanctification? We must yield ourselves completely to God

(Romans 6:13,19). We must purify our lives (2 Corinthians 7:1). We must read God's Word, for by His truth we are sanctified (John 17:17). We must walk in obedience to the Spirit and not fulfill the lust of the flesh (Galatians 5:16-18).

In the New Testament all Christians are called saints (Romans 1:7; 2 Corinthians 1:1; Ephesians 1:1). This word *saints* (*hagios*) comes from the same Greek words that are translated *sanctification* (*hagiosune, hagiosmos*). It is also the same adjective used in referring to the *Holy* Spirit. We were sanctified when we were saved; now we must with the help of the Holy Spirit demonstrate by our lives that we are truly separated from sin and dedicated to God.

The Baptism in the Holy Spirit

In the 20th century millions of earnest believers have experienced the baptism in the Holy Spirit just as the disciples did on the Day of Pentecost (Acts 2:4).

Historically speaking, the Day of Pentecost was the birth date of the Church. God poured out His Spirit on the early believers to enable them to witness effectively and spread the gospel to the ends of the earth (1:8).

But the Day of Pentecost also has personal significance for every believer. It means that every Christian can be filled with the Spirit in the same way as the disciples in Jerusalem. The distinctive teaching of the Pentecostal Movement is this baptism in the Holy Spirit, which is accompanied by speaking in tongues. Most non-Pentecostal Christians do not recognize the personal significance of Pentecost, regarding it only as a once-for-all historical event. Because of this they either reject the need for a personal baptism in the Spirit, or else they reject speaking in tongues as the Spirit gives utterance as the initial evidence of this baptism.

Is It the Same as Salvation?

Some believe the baptism in the Holy Spirit is the same as the work of the Holy Spirit in salvation. This teaching is that there is no separate experience in which a Christian is filled with the Holy Spirit subsequent to the experience of salvation.

Some of the misunderstanding comes from an incorrect interpretation of 1 Corinthians 12:13 which says: "For by one Spirit are we all baptized into one body." These people maintain that this is the same baptism as the one spoken of by John the Baptist when he said Christ would baptize in the Holy Spirit (Matthew 3:11). Now it is true that when we are saved we do receive the Holy Spirit as well (see Romans 8:16; Galatians 4:6). The Holy Spirit comes to regenerate us and to help us in our Christian walk. But when we speak of the baptism in the Holy Spirit, we are talking about another experience with the Holy Spirit.

In 1 Corinthians 12:13 the Holy Spirit baptizes us into the body of Christ. This is salvation. But in passages like Matthew 3:11, Christ baptizes us in the Holy Spirit. This happens *after* salvation. In other words, we are talking about two experiences—one a baptism *by* the Holy Spirit and another a baptism *in* the Holy Spirit.

The distinction between the Holy Spirit's work in salvation and this work is clearly illustrated in the New Testament. Philip preached in Samaria, with the result that many believed in Christ and were baptized in water (Acts 8:12). But these Samaritans did not at that time receive the fullness of the Holy Spirit, for we are told that Peter and John went from

Jerusalem to Samaria to lay their hands on the Samaritan believers that they might receive this fullness (vv. 14-17).

In Acts 19 we see the apostle Paul in Ephesus asking a group of disciples if they had received the Holy Spirit since they believed (v. 2). These disciples had an inadequate understanding of Jesus. Paul instructed them and baptized them in water in the name of the Lord Jesus. After this, he laid his hands on them and the Holy Spirit came upon them (vv. 5,6).

In both these instances we see a clear distinction between salvation and receiving the fullness of the Holy Spirit. This is why we say the baptism in the Holy Spirit is an experience subsequent to the experience of salvation.

Is It the Same as Sanctification?

Many who believe sanctification is a second definite work of grace say the experience may also be called the baptism in the Holy Spirit. They maintain that at this experience of sanctification the person is filled with the Holy Spirit. But it is strange that nowhere in the New Testament can we find any record of someone who was "sanctified." Furthermore, nowhere does the New Testament relate the baptism in the Holy Spirit to a so-called second definite work of grace.

Nevertheless, we must be careful we do not forget that we are talking about a baptism in the *Holy* Spirit. We saw previously that one of the major works of the Holy Spirit is the sanctification of believers on a continuing basis. We remember that on the Day of Pentecost "there appeared unto them cloven tongues like as of fire, and it sat upon each of them" (Acts 2:3). The symbol of fire is used throughout the

Scriptures to signify purification, and it is often linked with God's holiness.

You remember the promise was that believers would be baptized in the Holy Spirit *and fire* (Matthew 3:11). In other words, when we are baptized in the Holy Spirit we find it easier to live a God-pleasing life because of the new power of the Holy Spirit that has been given to us. But this is different from saying it represents *the* experience of sanctification, much less that it completely eradicates the cause of sin in our lives.

Our friends in Pentecostal churches that teach sanctification as a second definite work reject the view that it is the same as the baptism in the Holy Spirit. We enjoy close fellowship with these friends because we agree with them that the baptism in the Holy Spirit is not the same as the experience of salvation and that it is an experience subsequent to regeneration. With these friends it is probably correct to say that more binds us together than separates us in our view of the Holy Spirit's work.

Is Speaking in Tongues Necessary?

Even before the Pentecostal outpouring of the Spirit at the beginning of our century, some prominent leaders in the evangelical world taught that there was an experience subsequent to salvation called the baptism in the Holy Spirit. These men did not accept the Holiness view that it was the same as sanctification. But they did not accept the view, either, that the experience would be accompanied by speaking in tongues. Many Christians today believe in a baptism in the Holy Spirit after salvation, but they reject the teaching that a person will speak in tongues at the time of this baptism.

We notice in Acts 2:4 that *all* the disciples were

filled with the Holy Spirit and *all* spoke in tongues. As far as God was concerned, the speaking in tongues was not optional. He ordained that everyone would speak in tongues.

When Peter preached to the household of Cornelius and they accepted his message, we are told that the Holy Spirit fell on all of them. Some of Peter's Jewish-Christian friends were amazed at what had happened. They recognized that God had poured out the Holy Spirit on the Gentiles also. How did they know that the Gentiles had also been baptized in the Holy Spirit? Acts 10:46 says: "*For* they heard them speak with tongues, and magnify God." Speaking in tongues also accompanied the fullness of the Spirit some years later at Ephesus (19:6).

It is not necessary for the Book of Acts to state every time that persons who received the fullness of the Spirit spoke in tongues. What we have already noted is that this was the pattern God established.

9

How Should We Be Guided?

Just a short while ago I dressed myself for the day. What would be your opinion of me if I told you that before selecting each item of clothing I prayed that God would guide me, and that I followed this routine every day? I would pray about which suit, which shirt, which tie, which socks, which shoes.

Then what would be your opinion if I told you that that is not really the way I dress myself? What I really do is to pick a suit at random, put on the first shirt I see, close my eyes and pull a tie off the rack, open the dresser drawer and pick the two socks closest to my hand, then reach for any pair of footwear—even if it happened to be sneakers!

Your opinion, I hope, is that both approaches are very extreme. You would say something like, "For some things God expects us to use our common sense." Yet the two approaches represent two extremes people often use to try to determine God's will for their lives or for a particular situation. Many people feel insecure because they are not certain concerning what the future holds.

Christians and non-Christians alike are sometimes tempted to try to learn about the future by some questionable means. In this chapter we want to discuss how we can be guided and some of the false means of guidance some people follow.

How God Guides

God has wonderfully provided a number of means for guiding His children in making decisions. Most of the time these means work in connection with one another, but we will list them separately.

1. *By His Word.* God has given us His written Word—the Bible. It is God's clear revelation of His will for us. The Psalmist wrote: "Thy word is a lamp unto my feet, and a light unto my path" (Psalm 119: 105). When God has clearly stated something in His Word, it is improper for us to ask whether it is His will. For instance, God's Word clearly says, "Thou shalt not steal." Therefore it would be wrong for a person to wonder whether God might not excuse stealing in some circumstances.

A Christian man once made the statement that the Lord had told him to divorce his wife and marry another woman. This man's wife was a God-fearing woman; she was a good wife and mother; she was true to her husband. Yet he insisted it was God's will for him to divorce her. But the Lord Jesus himself spoke plainly against divorce (see Matthew 5:32). God does not contradict himself. He does not say one thing in His Word, and then tell us to do something contrary to it. We must always remember that "all Scripture is given by inspiration of God, and is profitable for doctrine, for reproof, for correction, for instruction in righteousness" (2 Timothy 3:16).

2. *By the Holy Spirit.* God's children are those who are led by His Spirit (Romans 8:14). A very interesting incident is found in Acts 16:6-10. The apostle Paul was on a missionary journey. He had a strong desire to evangelize the province of Asia. But he and his companions "were forbidden of the Holy Ghost to preach the word in Asia."

It was a very understandable desire on the part of

Paul. The city of Ephesus was in this province. It was a major city of the Roman Empire. He wanted the Ephesians to hear the gospel. But God had something else in mind. It was not that God opposed Paul's going to that area, for we read that on a later trip he did go to Ephesus and established a strong church in that city. It was simply not God's will for Paul to go at that particular time.

Paul then wished to go to the north through the province of Bithynia. But again the Spirit checked him. He had been on a westerly course when he was checked both times by the Holy Spirit. God wished him to continue heading west. At the city of Troas he received the vision of the man in Macedonia calling for help. The vision itself did not provide guidance for Paul. He accepted the vision because it harmonized with what the Holy Spirit had already impressed upon him. We must remember that visions and dreams must be evaluated by the Word of God and the witness of the Holy Spirit.

How can we know when the Holy Spirit is telling us not to follow a certain course of action? Most Christians can testify that if God has not clearly revealed His will by any other means they will experience an inner unrest over a decision they are about to make. Since all Christians have the Holy Spirit dwelling in them the Holy Spirit is faithful to guide us in the right path.

3. *By prayer.* Often it is while we are in an attitude of prayer that God speaks to us. This thought is closely connected with the previous thought of being guided by the Holy Spirit. In Acts 13 we read about certain men in the church who were praying and fasting. During that time the Holy Spirit spoke to them to send out Barnabas and Saul for the work to which the Lord had called them (vv. 1-3). We

are not told the manner in which the Holy Spirit spoke to them. It may have been by some kind of inner voice telling them what the will of God was.

It is well for us always to be in an attitude of prayer so God may give direction to our lives and help us make the right decisions. At times we must make an impending decision a special matter of prayer. But in the normal course of events, we may be sure that as we maintain an openness to the Holy Spirit and remain in an attitude of prayer, God will help us to know His will.

4. *By circumstances.* God often lets us know His will by the way He arranges different circumstances in our lives. The Lord is the One "that openeth, and no man shutteth; and shutteth, and no man openeth" (Revelation 3:7). He is the One who said: "I have set before thee an open door, and no man can shut it" (v. 8). He is the One who orders the steps of a good man (Psalm 37:23).

The apostle Paul was guided by circumstances. He wrote: "I will tarry at Ephesus until Pentecost. For a great door and effectual is opened unto me" (1 Corinthians 16:8,9). Paul had the conviction that as he sought to live in obedience to God, whatever happened to him was part of God's will for his life (Philippians 1:12,13).

I recently heard a missionary tell about his experiences in Africa. The government of the country in which he served was making it very difficult for Christians to spread the gospel. Immediately after a baptismal ceremony, two national pastors were arrested and imprisoned. When they were released and went to the missionary, the missionary indignantly said: "Brethren, we do not have to tolerate this kind of mistreatment by the government."

As he told this story to the congregation, he confessed how wrong he was, for the African pastors told him that he should not be disturbed over what had happened. During their imprisonment they were given wonderful opportunities to witness for the Lord Jesus Christ. Fellow prisoners and prison guards would never have heard the gospel if these two men had not been imprisoned!

Sometimes we have no control over the circumstances that come into our lives. During such times we simply take them as being from the Lord. But what do we do when we must choose between two or three options, each one of which is attractive and apparently in accordance with God's will? It is comforting to know that in these circumstances the Lord sometimes allows us to make the decision.

We must be careful never to make prayer a substitute for action. After we have prayed about a matter and sought the guidance of the Holy Spirit and still no answer is forthcoming, then perhaps the Lord is telling us to make the decision ourselves. He has endowed us with a mind which He expects us to use in evaluating situations.

5. *By authority and counsel.* We may be guided by instructions from those in authority over us, unless they conflict with the Word of God or our conscience. We should submit to the legitimate demands of government (Romans 13:1-6).

Some years ago a Lutheran bishop in East Germany was arrested for driving down the highway at excessive speed. Upon being questioned by the authorities, he insisted he was under no obligation to obey the speed laws of a godless, communistic government. Therefore he would travel at whatever speed he chose. But the bishop was mistaken. Any government has the legitimate authority to establish speed laws.

But the situation is different in the case of Peter. The authorities had told him not to teach in the name of Jesus. But Peter and the other apostles responded: "We ought to obey God rather than men" (Acts 5:28,29). They had been told to do something that was contrary to the Lord's command, and they refused to comply.

The same principle applies to other relationships with those in authority. We ought to be guided by sound instruction from spiritual overseers (Hebrews 13:7), and by decisions of fellow believers (Matthew 18:17). Children must be guided by parents, wives by husbands, employees by employers (Ephesians 5:22 to 6:9; Colossians 3:18 to 4:1). The basic instruction in all this is that this guidance must be "in the Lord"—meaning that it must be in accordance with God's will.

You must understand that God has a variety of ways by which He guides His people. As we investigate His Word, allow ourselves to be guided by His Spirit, think about the different options, are aware of the circumstances, and listen to proper authority, we can be assured that the Lord will be faithful in directing our paths.

In the remainder of this chapter we want to discuss how some people go astray by trying to obtain guidance or insight into the future. Two of these ways seem to have some basis in Scripture. Another two are definitely condemned in the Scriptures. We will examine them in turn.

What the Bible Seems to Say

1. *Guidance by prophetic utterances.* Some people place emphasis on the gift of prophecy as a means of

obtaining divine direction. Because the Pentecostal Movement believes in and encourages the operation of spiritual gifts, the Movement from its beginning has had people who place undue emphasis on gifts like prophecy.

Some very sincere people have been misled by what was supposed to be an utterance from the Lord. Also, some well-meaning people have given these prophecies, not realizing that what they said came from their own spirit and not from the Holy Spirit. We know instances of people who went to mission fields in response to a prophetic utterance that told them that as soon as they got to the field the Lord would miraculously give them the language of that country. These people, of course, were totally disillusioned when they discovered that they would have to study the language instead. Sometimes a "prophecy" said that two persons were to marry. But it turned out that the man and woman were ill-suited for each other, and some couples found this out too late.

This does not mean God does not communicate to His people by means of the gift of prophecy. We already talked about the incident in Acts 13 where the Spirit impressed upon the church leaders to separate Barnabas and Saul for missionary work. But notice that those two men had already been called by God and had already done missionary work. What happened at Antioch was more of a confirmation of God's call upon their lives.

We must remember that the primary purpose of the gift of prophecy is to build up, encourage, and comfort God's people (1 Corinthians 14:3). We are also told that prophecies must be evaluated: "Let the prophets speak two or three, and let the other judge" (v. 29). Above everything else, prophetic utterances must be evaluated in the light of the Word of God. Any prophecy that goes counter to His Word must be rejected.

2. *Guidance by fleeces and lots.* The story about Gideon and the fleece of wool is very familiar (Judges 6:36-40). Gideon wanted assurance from God that he would be victorious over his enemies. He put out the fleece, asking the Lord that the next morning the fleece be wet and the earth around it dry. God accommodated him. To be doubly sure, the next night he asked the Lord to keep the fleece dry and make the ground wet. Again God accommodated him. This is where we get the expression "putting out a fleece."

But notice two things concerning this incident. First, God had already promised Gideon victory over his enemies. The incident of the fleece was really an expression of doubt on Gideon's part. Second, nowhere are we told that this type of action ought to be practiced by God's people.

In Biblical times lots were also used to determine God's will. The casting of lots was used, for instance, to determine which goat was to be sacrificed on the Day of Atonement and which goat was to be released into the wilderness (see Leviticus 16:7-10). It was used in the New Testament by the disciples to determine who would be the successor of Judas (Acts 1:24-26). In some respects, the casting of lots could be likened to flipping a coin to help a person make a decision. But it was a method that was used and that God approved.

Are we justified today in following similar practices to determine God's will? Even though there is Biblical precedent for this, we should remember that it is basically an Old Testament practice. Lots were cast in the selection of Judas' successor, but that was before the outpouring of the Spirit on the Day of Pentecost. Nowhere after the outpouring of the Spirit do we read that the Early Church used lots to determine God's will. The reason is obvious. Since the Day of Pentecost God has given His Holy Spirit to all believers. One of the functions of the Holy Spirit is to guide God's people.

Means of Guidance Condemned by the Bible

The Word of God is very strong in denouncing certain practices used to determine divine guidance or to gain insight into the future. The two that come under special condemnation are astrology and the occult.

1. *Guidance by astrology*. The word *astrology* comes from two Greek words that together mean "a study of the stars." But this is misleading. Astrology is not a science. The science of the study of the stars is properly called *astronomy*.

Astrology is the belief that the positions of the heavenly bodies have an influence on human destiny. According to astrologers, future events are already determined by the positions of the stars and planets. Therefore, they say that a study of the positions of these bodies, especially their positions at the moment of a person's birth, will give guidance to the person for the future.

In the United States a recent poll indicates that as many as 32 million people take astrology seriously. Approximately 77 percent of the population know the astrological sign of the zodiac associated with their birthday. Why does astrology seem to be so popular? In a recent statement by some scientists, it was said: "In these uncertain times, many long for the comfort of having guidance in making decisions."

When we investigate some of the counsel given by

astrology, we notice that it is extremely general in nature. As a point of interest, I checked last night's paper which contained the daily horoscope. My horoscope for the day on which I am writing this chapter says: "Associates and co-workers may not all be heading in the same direction or acting for the same reasons. Think well before joining any side but, once decided, don't waver." You can readily see how noncommittal and general this is. Approximately 1 out of every 12 persons in the world has been given the same advice for this day.

Astrology is not logically consistent. If future events are already determined by the positions of the heavenly bodies, then it is meaningless to seek guidance. The idea of guidance implies the possibility of making a choice.

Christians cannot believe in astrology. God is the Creator of this universe and He controls it. He works together all things for good to those who love Him (Romans 8:28).

Astrology is as old as ancient Babylonia. Does it work? The astrologers in Nebuchadnezzar's court were unable to interpret his dream; but Daniel predicted the future because of his dependence on God (Daniel 2:27,28).

Listen to the very strong words of Isaiah the prophet directed to the astrologers of Babylon who were not able to foresee the destruction of the city: "Let now the astrologers, the stargazers, the monthly prognosticators, stand up, and save thee from these things that shall come upon thee. Behold, . . . they shall not deliver themselves from the power of the flame" (Isaiah 47:13,14). The astrologers were not able to foresee their own future, but Isaiah, under the inspiration of the Holy Spirit, could look 200 years ahead and prophesy even the name of Babylon's conqueror, Cyrus (see Isaiah 44:28; 45:1).

2. *Guidance by the occult.* Fortune-tellers and spiritist mediums are very popular today because they claim the power of foretelling the future. Often, especially with spiritist mediums, the reason for this claim is that they are in contact with the dead or other inhabitants of the spirit world.

God forbids any contact with fortune-tellers and mediums. Occultism was not new in Biblical times. Deuteronomy 18:10-12 says: "There shall not be found among you any . . . that useth divination, or an observer of times, or an enchanter, or a witch, or a charmer, or a consulter with familiar spirits, or a wizard, or a necromancer. For all that do these things are an abomination unto the LORD." Such people were to be put to death (see Leviticus 20:27). Israelites who consulted these people were also under divine judgment (v. 6).

King Saul is a tragic example of this (see 1 Samuel 28:7-25). He consulted the witch of Endor because God had departed from him.

The New Testament also contains prohibitions against contact with the occult. Galatians 5:20 lists witchcraft as one of the works of the flesh. The demon-possessed girl in Philippi had a spirit of divination, which Paul cast out (Acts 16:16-18). And the final destiny of sorcerers is the lake of fire (Revelation 21:8; 22:15).

10

The Security of the Believer

Can a Christian ever be lost? Is it possible for a person who once knew the Lord to forfeit his salvation? Many Christians answer with a very emphatic, "No." They say that under no conditions is it ever possible for a born-again believer to be lost. This doctrine is sometimes called "unconditional eternal security." It can be described as "once in grace, always in grace" or "once saved, always saved." It is the official position of almost all Presbyterian churches, the Reformed churches, and many Baptist churches.

What Does the Bible Say?

The doctrine of unconditional eternal security is contrary to the teaching of the Scriptures. Let us see how the Bible answers the question: "Can a Christian be lost?"

1. *Warnings of the Old and New Testaments.* In the Book of Ezekiel we read: "When the righteous turneth away from his righteousness, and committeth iniquity, and doeth according to all the abominations that the wicked man doeth, shall he live? All his righteousness that he hath done shall not be mentioned: in his trespass that he hath trespassed, and in his sin that he hath sinned, in them shall he die"

(18:24). Jeremiah says: "Cursed be the man, . . . whose heart departeth from the Lord" (17:5).

The Book of Hebrews also contains clear warnings. When a person tramples underfoot the blood of Christ by turning away from Him and insults the Holy Spirit, he can expect nothing but God's judgment (10:29). The possibility of drawing back is always present (vv. 38,39). Persons who turn away from Christ identify themselves with those who crucified Him (6:6). As long as they remain in that state, it is impossible for them to be saved.

Defenders of the "once saved, always saved" doctrine admit that the Bible contains very serious warnings. But they say the warnings are there only to motivate Christians to live a godly life and not to frighten them with the possibility of losing their salvation. They are not logical at this point. Warnings are given only when there is the possibility or presence of danger. Wouldn't it be ridiculous to have a railroad crossing sign in the Antarctic, where there are no trains?

2. *The example of Israel.* In the New Testament the Church is often compared with Israel. Paul even uses Israel as an example for the Church, and says that God will treat the Church in the same way He treated Israel if the Church acts as Israel did. He likens Israel to the branches of an olive tree. But he says that some of the branches were broken off because of unbelief (Romans 11:20). Then he gives this warning to Christians: "For if God spared not the natural branches, take heed lest he also spare not thee" (v. 21)

Jesus himself said: "Every branch in me that beareth not fruit he taketh away" (John 15:2). He added: "If a man abide not in me, he is cast forth as a branch, and is withered; and men gather them, and cast them into the fire, and they are burned" (v. 6).

3. *The "if" clauses.* The New Testament teaches *conditional* eternal security. A believer is secure only when he meets certain conditions. Many of these conditions are in the form of "if" clauses. We already mentioned one stated by Jesus.

Here is one from Peter: "If after they have escaped the pollutions of the world through the knowledge of the Lord and Saviour Jesus Christ, they are again entangled therein, and overcome, the latter end is worse with them than the beginning. For it had been better for them not to have known the way of righteousness, than, after they have known it, to turn from the holy commandment delivered unto them" (2 Peter 2:20,21).

Paul says that Christ will present Christians holy, unblamable, and unreprovable in God's sight "if ye continue in the faith grounded and settled, and be not moved away from the hope of the gospel" (Colossians 1:22,23). He also says: "For if ye live after the flesh, ye shall die: but if ye through the Spirit do mortify the deeds of the body, ye shall live" (Romans 8:13).

4. *Faith as a constant requirement.* In New Testament Greek, the present tense of a verb refers to a continuing action rather than a once-for-all action. With this in mind, we can correctly translate John 3:16 this way: "For God so loved the world, that He gave His only begotten Son, that whosoever keeps on believing in Him should not perish, but should continue to have eternal life."

It is not enough to have believed in Christ at one time; we must continue to believe in Him to continue receiving spiritual life. Paul echoes the same thought when he says: "Because of unbelief they [Israel] were broken off, and thou standest by faith" (Romans 11:20).

5. *The categorical statements of Scripture.* One of the most devastating statements against the "once in grace, always in grace" position is found in Galatians 5:4, which says: "Christ is become of no effect unto you, whosoever of you are justified by the law; ye are fallen from grace." How can people fall from a place where they have never been? People can fall from grace only if they are in grace.

An amusing, and yet tragic, incident occurred during my graduate theological studies at a Lutheran seminary. We were studying the Book of Galatians and the professor was reading the first part of chapter 5. As soon as he read the words, "Ye are fallen from grace," a Presbyterian student waved his hand frantically. The professor asked if he had a comment, to which this student replied, "That can't mean what it seems to mean!" Unfortunately, he could not accept a clear statement from Scripture because it contradicted his theology.

The Extreme View of Unconditional Eternal Security

The defenders of this doctrine justify it on the basis of the following arguments:

1. *We receive eternal life from God.* If this life is eternal, then, they maintain, it is never-ending—it is the eternal possession of Christians. But this argument cannot stand up. The idea of eternal life existed long before any of us were saved. It may be likened to a river that flows eternally. When we are converted, God places us in that stream of eternal life. But it is possible for a person to remove himself from the stream. Eternal life is not affected, but his participation in that eternal life may be affected.

I once had a pen with a lifetime guarantee. The manufacturers gave the assurance that it would last for my entire lifetime. But the guarantee also included a statement that the manufacturer would not be held responsible if the pen was deliberately abused or misused. Furthermore, the manufacturer could do nothing for me if I lost the pen. The guarantee would still be valid, but under those conditions I could not benefit by it. So it is with eternal life. There is nothing wrong with God's guarantee of eternal life, but we must be careful not to do anything to nullify that guarantee.

2. *Scriptural statements say it is impossible to be separated from God.* Defenders of this doctrine often point to Jesus' words in John 10:28,29, which read: "And I give unto them eternal life; and they shall never perish, neither shall any man pluck them out of my hand. My Father, which gave them me, is greater than all; and no man is able to pluck them out of my Father's hand."

They also point to Paul's words in Romans 8:35-39 which stress that no one or nothing is able to separate us from the love of God. Paul himself had experienced many of the things he lists in those verses, and he knew from those experiences that none of them could separate him from Christ. But notice that in both Jesus' and Paul's statements, the assurance is that nothing *outside* of ourselves can ever separate us from the Lord. These passages say nothing about something *inside* us—our own will and desires—separating us from the Lord.

Defenders of this erroneous doctrine accuse their opponents of not having enough faith in God's keeping power. We agree with them and the apostle Paul on this matter, for Paul says: "Being confident of this very thing, that he which hath begun a good work

in you will perform it until the day of Jesus Christ"
(Philippians 1:6). It is not a question of God's keeping power, but of our willingness to have God keep us.

3. *Nothing a son does will ever change his status as a son.* This sounds like a plausible argument. According to this teaching, no matter what a son does he will never cease to be his father's son. So once we become a child of God, it is impossible for us ever to be anything else. In other words, a person cannot be "unborn."

In response to this argument, we can say that at one time we were sons of disobedience (Ephesians 2:2). We were the devil's children. But it was possible for us to change our status and become God's children. By an act of our will we changed our status. In the same way, it is possible for a child of God to change his status and once again become a child of the devil.

Even in the everyday world about us, a son can fall into disfavor with his father and be completely disinherited and disowned. Furthermore, the son has the power to reject his heritage. But the proponents of this false doctrine actually say that once a person is saved he is stripped of his free will. Whether he likes it or not, he will always remain a child of God.

4. *If some people go back to a life of open sin, this means they were never saved in the first place.* This is the viewpoint of some who hold the unconditional eternal security doctrine. They say it is possible for a person to go through the motions of becoming a Christian without really having a change of heart. They tell us that such people may appear to have changed for a while, but the fact that they go back into sin shows they were not really born again.

We cannot argue against the idea that some people may outwardly appear to be Christians without having had a change of heart. But this is a very convenient way some eternal-security people have of dismissing what they know is a genuine theological problem for them. If what they say is true, then no one can have the assurance of salvation because there will always be the possibility of going back to a life of sin, which according to them means the person was never saved.

5. *Unconditional eternal security is based on the doctrine of divine election.* This doctrine is taught by the followers of John Calvin—all the Reformed churches and almost all the Presbyterian churches. Their view of divine election, or predestination, is that God chooses certain persons to be saved and then gives them saving faith. Those whom He has not chosen are lost. This choice by God is a sovereign one; it is not based on whether God foreknows if a person will repent and believe.

We respond to this by saying it is the reverse of what the Bible teaches. The Bible says: "Believe on the Lord Jesus Christ, and thou shalt be saved" (Acts 16:31); not: "Be saved, and thou shalt believe on the Lord Jesus Christ." Faith comes first, then salvation.

Furthermore, this teaching of Calvinism deprives man of any free will in matters pertaining to salvation. It teaches that if God has chosen someone to be saved, that person will be saved whether he wants to or not. This is sometimes called irresistible grace. But again we must disagree on the basis of Biblical teaching. The Bible shows that men continually resist God's grace. Stephen said to his persecutors: "Ye stiffnecked and uncircumcised in heart and ears, ye do always resist the Holy Ghost: as your fathers did, so do ye" (7:51).

Conditional vs. Unconditional Security

You must be clear on the distinction between conditional security and unconditional security. Conditional security teaches that God is able to keep His children from falling (Jude 24). But it also places responsibility on the believer to keep himself in the love of God (v. 21). On the other hand, unconditional security teaches that no matter what a person does after he is saved, he will never forfeit his salvation. You can see what a dangerous doctrine this is.

Prior to joining the United States Navy I knew about this doctrine of unconditional eternal security but had not met many people who believed it. I was shocked when I discovered that some young men in my boot-camp company who professed to be Christians were living very ungodly lives. They used profanity, got drunk, and indulged in sexual immorality. I asked one of them how he could be a Christian. He said he had received Christ as his Saviour when he was 12 years old, and that meant he would never lose his salvation.

Our response to this is based on the Word of God. In Galatians 5:19-21 Paul lists the works of the flesh. Among these he includes adultery, fornication, uncleanness, lasciviousness, drunkenness, and revelings. Then he concludes with the statement: "They which do such things shall not inherit the kingdom of God." Revelation 21:8 also says that those who practice these things "shall have their part in the lake which burneth with fire and brimstone."

We reject the extreme view of unconditional eternal security, but we must be careful not to go to the opposite extreme which could be called conditional eternal *insecurity*. We must not preoccupy ourselves with the thought of losing our salvation. The Christian life is one of joy and peace in the Lord. The warnings in Scripture about falling away are not meant to frighten the believer into insecurity. Thank God, "If we walk in the light, as he [God himself] is in the light, . . . the blood of Jesus Christ his Son cleanseth us from all sin" (1 John 1:7).

11

What's Ahead for the Unbeliever?

Everybody gets resurrected! The resurrection of the dead includes both Christians and non-Christians. When the Lord Jesus Christ returns, the "dead in Christ" will rise first (1 Thessalonians 4:16,17). At that time their bodies will become incorruptible (1 Corinthians 15:53).

But the Bible also talks about the resurrection of the wicked dead. Jesus taught that all who are in the grave will one day hear His voice and come forth: "They that have done good, unto the resurrection of life; and they that have done evil, unto the resurrection of damnation" (John 5:29). In the Book of Revelation we read about the Great White Throne Judgment when the dead will stand before God. "And whosoever was not found written in the book of life was cast into the lake of fire" (20:15).

The most solemn truth in all the Bible is that sin will be punished. But punishment does not always come in this life. Sometimes the most ungodly people have a life full of comfort and ease. They don't seem to lack anything in the way of this world's goods. Some, in spite of their ungodly ways, enjoy good health and long life.

On the other hand, some very godly people suffer much in this life. But a Christian has the glorious hope of the resurrection from the dead and spending eternity in the presence of the Lord. It will be an existence free from all want and suffering. How different from the eternal future that awaits those who reject God's offer of salvation in this life!

When Does Punishment Begin?

Punishment for sin begins immediately after death. Jesus taught this clearly in the story about the rich man and Lazarus (Luke 16:19-31). The rich man died and was buried, "and in hell he lifted up his eyes, being in torments" (v. 23). Just as Christians immediately upon death go to be with the Lord, so the ungodly immediately upon death go to a place of torment. The thought of eternal punishment is not pleasant, but it is the teaching of God's Word.

The Bible uses a number of terms when it talks about the place to which people go when they die. In the Old Testament the Hebrew word *Sheol* (shee-OLE) occurs more than 60 times. It is often translated "hell" or "grave." However, the translation "hell" is unfortunate because the word simply refers to the abode of the dead. Both the godly and the ungodly go to *Sheol*.

In the New Testament we find the Greek word *Hades* (HAY-deez). The meaning is the same as that for *Sheol*—the abode of the dead. Neither of these words refers to eternal punishment, even though the wicked dead suffer while in Hades. Unfortunately, some versions translate this word as "hell." This is the case in the story about the rich man being in "hell." It should really read: "And in Hades he lifted up his eyes, being in torments."

The New Testament word that should properly be translated "hell" is *Gehenna* (Ge-HEN-na). The name has a Hebrew origin and means Valley of Hinnom, which was located outside the city of Jerusalem. In Old Testament times it was the center of the idolatrous worship of the god Molech, to whom children were sacrificed by fire (2 Chronicles 28:3; 33:6). King Josiah abolished these sacrifices and defiled the site, so that in subsequent years his action was associated with the judgment to come upon God's disobedient people (Jeremiah 7:32).

The word *Gehenna* occurs 12 times in the New Testament (Matthew 5:22,29,30; 10:28; 18:9; 23:15, 33; Mark 9:43,45,47; Luke 12:5; James 3:6). In all the passages it refers to the place of eternal punishment for the wicked. What surprises many people is that the Lord Jesus Christ used this word more than anyone else in the New Testament.

Gehenna was the "city dump" of Jerusalem. It was used to dispose of refuse, dead animals, and the bodies of criminals. Fires burned continually to consume all the waste and filth of the city. This is why Jesus used it as a figure of speech for the place of eternal punishment. He said it was the place where both body and soul will be punished (Matthew 10: 28). He spoke of it as a place where existence continues and where the fire is never extinguished (Mark 9:46; Matthew 23:33).

The *lake of fire* is another name for hell (Revelation 20:14). It is also called the lake of fire and brimstone (20:10; compare 19:20; 21:8). Satan, Antichrist, and the false prophet will be cast into it. This is what Jesus referred to when he spoke of "everlasting fire, prepared for the devil and his angels" (Matthew 25:41). He also talked about a furnace of fire (13:41,42,49,50). The sad commentary of Scripture is that even though the lake of fire was originally planned for Satan and his angels, it must also be the eternal abode of all who choose to follow him (Revelation 21:8).

Because the doctrine of eternal punishment is so distasteful to many people, a number of erroneous teachings are held concerning the nature of the punishment. We will now look at the most commonly held views.

Annihilation of the Wicked Dead

This is the official teaching of the Seventh-Day Adventists and Jehovah's Witnesses. They hold that the righteous dead will enjoy a state of blessedness forever, but that the wicked dead will be annihilated —their existence will be obliterated. But the Bible clearly rejects this teaching.

In the New Testament the same Greek expression is used to talk about both eternal life and eternal punishment. Matthew 25:46 is one example: "And these shall go away into everlasting [*eis aionion*] punishment: but the righteous into life eternal [*eis aionion*]." (There is no difference in meaning between the English words *eternal* and *everlasting*.)

If the duration of the righteous person's life is eternal or everlasting, then the duration of the unrighteous person's existence is also eternal or everlasting. It is totally inconsistent to say that eternal life is unending but eternal punishment will have an end.

Another Scripture passage is very positive about this. Revelation 20:10 speaks about the devil being cast into the lake of fire and brimstone, where he "shall be tormented day and night for ever and ever."

Some false teachers say that annihilation is meant when the Bible talks about the "second death" (20: 14; 21:8). But they do not really understand the Biblical meaning of the word *death*. Its basic meaning is separation. Physical death means the separation of the soul from the body. Spiritual death means separation from fellowship with God (Ephesians 2: 1). Eternal death, or the second death, means eternal separation from God. Tragically, much of the torment of hell will be that eternally lost men and women will realize they are forever cut off from the presence of God.

Jehovah's Witnesses, contrary to the teaching of Scripture, talk about "the God-dishonoring doctrine of a fiery hell for tormenting conscious human souls eternally" (*Let God Be True*, [Brooklyn: Watchtower Bible and Tract Society, 2nd rev. ed., 1952], p. 88). In the same publication they say that "Gehenna . . . is a picture or symbol of complete annihilation, and not of eternal torment" (p. 97).

What do they do with the story of the rich man and Lazarus? We already saw that it clearly says the rich man was tormented by the flames. They very conveniently say it is a parable, and therefore cannot be taken literally. According to them, this parable is a prophecy that has been undergoing fulfillment since 1919. The rich man represents "the clergy of Christendom" who are far from God and are being tormented by the truth being proclaimed by Jehovah's Witnesses. Lazarus is the faithful remnant of the body of Christ (Jehovah's Witnesses, of course!) who are being comforted by the truth of God's Word. Isn't it remarkable how far some people will go to twist the meaning of Scripture simply because they refuse to accept its clear teachings?

Is the idea of hell repugnant? Of course it is! That is why God gave His only begotten Son, His most treasured possession, so those who believe in Him would not perish but have everlasting life (John 3:16). God does not really "send" anyone to hell. But because some men have chosen in this life to reject Christ and to follow Satan, they then follow

Satan also to the place prepared for him and his angels.

A Second Chance

Some erroneously teach that God will give the unsaved a chance to repent after they die, and thus enable them to transfer from hell to heaven. Many base this argument on human reasoning, saying that a God of love would not condemn someone eternally for a decision he made in this life. But others try to base this belief on some isolated Scripture verses. Let us look at them.

First Peter 3:19 says that Jesus went and preached to the spirits in prison. According to this false teaching, when Jesus died His spirit went to the region of the dead where He preached the gospel to the ungodly to give them another chance to be saved.

Even the best Bible scholars disagree as to when this "preaching" took place. Some say it refers to Jesus' preaching through the Holy Spirit to the ungodly in Noah's time. Others say it refers to Jesus' activity in the spirit during the 3-day interval between His death and resurrection. If this is the correct interpretation, it still does not say that He preached *the gospel* to those disobedient spirits of the wicked dead. The Greek verb used here is *kerusso,* which simply means "to make a proclamation." We do not know what the proclamation was about, but it certainly is going too far to say it means the gospel. The verb *evangelizomai* means "to preach the gospel," but that is not the word Peter uses in this verse.

The second passage is 1 Peter 4:6, which says the gospel was preached "to them that are dead." In this verse Peter uses the word *evangelizomai,* "to preach the gospel." But notice that the verse does not say this preaching is now being done or that it will be done, but that it *was* done. When was it done? When they were alive! These people will be judged "according to men *in the flesh.*"

Let me illustrate it this way. How would you understand it if I said, "My late (or dead) brother once heard Oral Roberts preach"? Would you take it to mean that the preaching took place after my brother had died? Of course not. The obvious meaning is that he heard the preaching while he was alive.

Furthermore, Jesus plainly said: "He that believeth not is condemned already" (John 3:18). If a person dies in that state, he is still condemned.

Again, the story of the rich man and Lazarus illustrates this point. Abraham said to the rich man who was in torment: "Between us and you there is a great gulf fixed: so that they which would pass from hence to you cannot; neither can they pass to us, that would come from thence" (Luke 16:26).

Death seals the state in which a person died. If, like Lazarus, he dies righteous, he is confirmed in righteousness; if, like the rich man, he dies wicked he is confirmed in his wickedness. We must remember the unqualified statement of Scripture: "It is appointed unto men once to die, but after this the judgment" (Hebrews 9:27).

Universalism

Universalism is the teaching that eventually all men will be saved. Some even go so far as to say even the devil will be saved in the end. Those who hold this teaching say that a God of love could not possibly condemn men to eternal punishment, even though they may concede that some kind of temporal punishment is necessary. They say it is a distorted view of God that makes men believe in everlasting punishment.

The teaching of universalism found its way into the Church as early as the third century through the church father Origen. It has always been taught by the Universalist Church, which united with the Unitarians to become the Unitarian-Universalist Association. It is held by many churches and groups that are doctrinally liberal. Traces of it may also be found in some evangelical circles.

A favorite passage of universalists is a part of Acts 3:21 which speaks about "the times of restitution of all things." According to many of them, the wicked who go to the lake of fire will eventually be purified, thus making them fit for heaven. The lake of fire may be likened to a purgatory for the wicked dead, just as the purgatory of the Roman Catholic Church is for the righteous dead. But this verse does not refer to Satan and the wicked dead. It is talking about Creation, which will be restored to its original state but which now, because of Adam's sin, has been "made subject to vanity, not willingly" (Romans 8:20).

Another line of reasoning followed by universalists is that Christ died for all, therefore all will be saved. Otherwise, they say, it detracts from His redemptive work on the cross. In response to this we must distinguish between the *sufficiency* and *efficiency* of the death of Jesus. It was sufficient for all mankind, but it is efficient or effective only for those who repent and believe.

One passage that completely devastates the doctrine of universalism is Matthew 12:32, which says: "Whosoever speaketh against the Holy Ghost, it shall not be forgiven him, neither in this world, neither in the world to come." If even one person cannot be forgiven, then it is impossible for *all* men to be reconciled to God.

Reincarnation

This doctrine is related to the "second chance" and universalist teachings, but it is different enough to receive separate attention. It is held by religious groups in this country whose teachings are traceable to oriental philosophy and religions. Among them are Zen Buddhism, Unity, and more recent groups that follow Indian gurus or teachers. This doctrine is stated clearly in Unity's *Statement of Faith,* part 22:

> We believe that the dissolution of spirit, soul, and body caused by death is annulled by rebirth of the same spirit and soul in another body here on earth. We believe the repeated incarnations of man to be a merciful provision of our loving Father to the end that all may have opportunity to attain immortality through regeneration as did Jesus.

This doctrine of reincarnation is completely removed from anything in Scripture. There is nothing in the Bible that even remotely suggests the possibility of any such existences. What we have already seen in responding to other false doctrines holds true here. There is no second (or third, or fourth) chance after death. Death confirms either a person's righteous state or his wicked state, inasmuch as it is appointed to men to die once, after which they experience God's judgment.

12

What's Ahead for the Believer?

When Adam sinned, death entered the world (Romans 5:12). Every coffin, every grave, is a grim reminder of the awful and far-reaching consequences of sin. Part of Adam's punishment for sin was physical death.

How should a Christian view death? The loss of a loved one is a very sobering experience. Even if the deceased person was a Christian, death involves temporary separation. But the sorrow manifested by Christians upon the death of a fellow Christian is totally different from the despair, hopelessness, and resignation often manifested by those who do not know the Lord. When a Christian loved one or friend dies, we have the glorious prospect of reunion someday. No such hope characterizes those who do not know the Lord.

A recently widowed woman was approached by an acquaintance who said, "I'm so sorry to learn that you lost your husband."

The widow, who was a Christian, responded, "Thank you for your concern, but I haven't lost him. I know exactly where he is. He is with the Lord."

Every religion has some kind of belief in life after death. But many of their views are erroneous when compared with the teachings of Scripture. We will now look at some of these erroneous teachings.

Do Christians Go Directly to Heaven?

When Christians die, they go immediately into the presence of the Lord. There is no waiting period. Jesus said to the repentant thief on the cross: "Today shalt thou be with me in paradise" (Luke 23:43). The apostle Paul said: "To die is gain" (Philippians 1:21). He went on to say he had a desire to depart "and to be with Christ" which was far better than remaining here on earth (v. 23). He said in another place: "We are . . . willing rather to be absent from the body, and to be present with the Lord" (2 Corinthians 5:8). Then, too, Jesus said that when Lazarus the beggar died the angels carried him into Abraham's bosom (Luke 16:22).

I remember well the words of one of my seminary professors who was a godly man with many years of pastoral experience. He was talking to our class about ministering to people who are on their deathbed. He said it was a tremendous source of comfort to such people to be told that as soon as they died they would not have to go on a long journey or wait a long time before being with the Lord. He always assured them they would go immediately into the presence of the Lord.

Even though a Christian does go immediately into God's presence upon death, his body remains on earth. But the time will come, when the Lord Jesus Christ returns, that our corruptible bodies will put on incorruption, and our mortal bodies will put on immortality (1 Corinthians 15:54). The resurrection of the body is a glorious prospect for the Christian, because it means his body will be reunited with his soul for all eternity.

What will our resurrected bodies be like? God will "transform the body of our humble state into conformity with the body of His [Christ's] glory, by the exertion of the power that He has even to subject all things to Himself" (Philippians 3:21, *NASB*).

The resurrection of Jesus from the dead insured our own resurrection. That is why Jesus could say: "I am the resurrection, and the life: he that believeth in me, though he were dead, yet shall he live" (John 11:25). The same Holy Spirit that quickened and transformed the lifeless body of Jesus in the tomb will do the same thing for us (Romans 8:11).

Since the resurrection bodies of believers will be like the glorified body of Jesus (Philippians 3:21; 1 John 3:2; 1 Corinthians 15:49), let us notice the following points from Scripture:

1. *The resurrection body of Jesus consisted of "flesh and bones"* (Luke 24:39). We may not understand exactly what this means, but it certainly tells us our resurrected bodies will be more than spiritual bodies.

2. *The resurrection body will be a spiritual body* (1 Corinthians 15:44). But we should not take this to mean that our resurrected bodies will not have any substance to them. What this probably means is that the source of life for the resurrection body will be the Holy Spirit, just as the life of our present physical bodies is the blood.

3. *The resurrection body will be incorruptible* (vv. 42,53,54). Our bodies will no longer be subject to weariness, sickness, or death.

Error Concerning the Doctrine of Purgatory

Purgatory is a Roman Catholic doctrine. The Roman Catholic Church teaches that very few people are worthy to go directly to heaven upon dying. The only ones who pass directly into God's presence are martyrs for the faith and faithful Catholics who perform sufficient good works in this life to offset their sins. All others who die "in a state of grace" must first go to purgatory. The Roman Catholic belief is that even though the death of Christ saves us from the eternal punishment of sin, we must still suffer temporally for our sins.

Purgatory is a place of preparation for heaven. While in purgatory the soul is cleansed of the effects of sins committed in this life.

This is another example of the Roman Catholic doctrine of faith plus works for salvation. The more good works a person performs in this life, the less time he will have to spend in purgatory.

The Roman Catholic Church teaches that there are a number of ways in which a person's stay in purgatory may be shortened. In addition to performing good works, a person may recite certain prayers for which he is granted an indulgence. An indulgence amounts to a reduction in the time a person must spend in purgatory. Sometimes it is stated in terms of so many days or months. In addition, masses may be said on behalf of the deceased person. These masses will also shorten his time in purgatory.

According to Roman Catholic teaching, a person can never know in this life whether he is saved. There is always the element of uncertainty which should drive a person to perform all these good works and say these prayers to lessen the time he will spend in purgatory. Furthermore, loved ones of a departed person can never be sure they have said enough prayers for him or have had enough masses celebrated for him. Even Pope John, on his deathbed, requested the prayers of the faithful as he passed from this life.

There is no foundation in Scripture for this doctrine of purgatory. Roman Catholics sometimes appeal to Matthew 12:32, which says: "Whosoever speaketh against the Holy Ghost, it shall not be forgiven him,

neither in this world, neither in the world to come."
They interpret this to mean there is forgiveness for
other sins in the world to come. But there is no
reference whatever to purgatory in this passage.
Jesus is simply saying that blasphemy against the
Holy Spirit is so serious that it has eternal consequences. This attitude toward the Holy Spirit puts a
person beyond God's grace.

Roman Catholics also appeal to 1 Corinthians
3:11-15. This passage talks about every man's works
being tried by fire, and verse 15 says: "If any man's
work shall be burned, he shall suffer loss: but
he himself shall be saved; yet so as by fire."

The traditional Roman Catholic view of purgatory
is that it is a place of cleansing by fire. (However,
the Roman Catholic Church distinguishes this from
hell.) But this passage refers to Christians appearing
before the judgment seat of Christ to be judged for
their works. Their works of wood, hay, and stubble
will be burned. But no mention is made that the soul
of the person itself will be purged. As we have already
seen, Christians who die go immediately into the
presence of the Lord.

The Investigative Judgment

The investigative judgment is a teaching of Seventh-
Day Adventism. This doctrine teaches that some time
in the 1840's Christ entered the heavenly Holy of
Holies to purify it and to begin the investigative
judgment. According to this teaching, the investigative judgment decides who of the tens of thousands
who have died are worthy to take part in the first
resurrection, and who of the living population are
worthy of being translated. In other words, Christ
moved into the heavenly Holy of Holies and took up
the work of evaluating the conduct of all people.

What does the Bible say concerning this? There is absolutely no Biblical basis for it. By holding this doctrine, Seventh-Day Adventism is guilty of legalism. The investigative judgment determines on the basis of a person's conduct whether he is prepared for eternity. But as we already saw in chapter 5, our salvation cannot depend on our good conduct. It is still by grace through faith, "and not of works" (Ephesians 2:8,9).

The Bible so clearly says: "He that believeth on him [Christ] is not condemned" (John 3:18). Jesus himself said: "He that heareth my word, and believeth on him that sent me, hath everlasting life, and shall not come into condemnation" (5:24). Then listen to the words of the apostle Paul: "There is therefore now no condemnation to them which are in Christ Jesus" (Romans 8:1).

Our sins are judged at the Cross. We already have eternal life. Any idea of an "investigative judgment" is contrary to the assurance of salvation which God gives to those who believe in His Son.

Soul Sleep

Jehovah's Witnesses and Seventh-Day Adventists teach the doctrine of "soul sleep." This doctrine says there is no consciousness during the intermediate state (the period between death and the resurrection of the body). Jehovah's Witnesses teach that when the wicked die, they die forever both physically and spiritually. According to them, the wicked dead are never raised from the dead to suffer eternal punishment. Seventh-Day Adventists differ by saying that all, believers and unbelievers, will be raised from the dead.

This teaching of soul sleep is connected with another teaching called "conditional immortality."

Conditional immortality teaches that only the righteous dead will live forever following the resurrection. According to this view, immortality is not a basic element in man. It is a gift God gives only to the saved at the time of their resurrection.

The teaching of soul sleep interprets literally the Biblical passages that refer to death as sleep. Jesus himself used the word *sleep* to mean death when He said concerning the daughter of the ruler of the synagogue: "The damsel is not dead, but sleepeth" (Mark 5:39). When referring to Lazarus' death, He again spoke of it as sleep (John 11:11). Even Jesus' death is referred to in this way by the apostle Paul when he says that Jesus has "become the firstfruits of them that slept" (1 Corinthians 15:20).

Paul goes on to say: "We shall not all sleep, but we shall all be changed" (v. 51). When the Lord returns to take His followers out of this world, the Bible says: "We who are alive, and remain until the coming of the Lord, shall not precede those who have fallen asleep" (1 Thessalonians 4:15, *NASB.*)

But Jehovah's Witnesses and Seventh-Day Adventists are mistaken when they place a literal meaning on the word *sleep.* One reason this word is used in referring to death is to suggest the temporary nature of death, inasmuch as all will be raised from the dead (John 5:28,29). The basic error of this teaching of soul sleep is that it applies the word *sleep* in a literal way to the *soul*, whereas the Bible uses it in a figurative way for the *body*.

Jesus certainly rejected this doctrine when He talked about Lazarus the beggar and the rich man (Luke 16:19-31). Immediately upon death Lazarus was carried by the angels into Abraham's bosom and the rich man found himself in torment. We know

Lazarus was conscious at this time because the rich man asked Abraham to send Lazarus to testify to his five brothers.

We remember again the words of Jesus to the repentant thief: "Today shalt thou be with me in paradise" (Luke 23:43). There is no suggestion here of a long term of unconsciousness before this man could enjoy fellowship with the Lord.

When we turn to the Book of Revelation, we read about the souls of martyrs which are in heaven. They are certainly conscious, for John hears them cry with a loud voice: "How long, O Lord, holy and true, dost thou not judge and avenge our blood on them that dwell on the earth?" (6:10).

When the Bible refers to death as sleep, we must also understand it to mean that it is the time when the soul is separated from the body. When we sleep, our bodies are not aware of anything that is taking place around us. But our subconscious minds are certainly active during sleep; this activity often taking the form of dreams. So it is with physical death. Our bodies have no awareness of what is taking place in the world, but our souls, the part of us that makes us aware of the spiritual world, are certainly active.

Marriage for Eternity

Marriage for eternity, or celestial marriage, is a peculiar doctrine of Mormonism. Mormonism distinguishes it from a marriage for time, in which the bond between husband and wife is broken at death. This kind of marriage has no validity for the life hereafter. Even though these people will be in a saved condition for all eternity, they will not be exalted. Exaltation, according to Mormon teaching, means that some faithful Mormons will become gods in the hereafter. But Mormons who were married in time can only hope to become angels of God for ever and ever (*Doctrines and Covenants* [Salt Lake City: Church of Jesus Christ of Latter-day Saints], 132:17).

Celestial marriage is very different. It is performed only in a Mormon temple. The details of the ceremony are never disclosed to outsiders. It seems that one of the primary purposes of this type of marriage is to bring new souls into the world.

Mormonism also teaches that there are three grades in heaven: the telestial, which is the lowest and where unbelievers seem to go; the terrestrial, which is for sincere but ignorant persons; and the celestial, which is for faithful Mormons.

These beliefs are far removed from anything the Bible suggests. Jesus made it clear that in heaven people neither marry nor are given in marriage (Luke 20:35). It seems that the Mormon belief of celestial marriage is based on an understanding of heaven that is mostly physical in nature. Believers will certainly have glorified bodies in heaven, but this does not mean our glorified bodies will perform the functions of our physical bodies. There is nothing in Scripture to suggest this.

While we read in the Bible that some Christians will suffer loss at the judgment seat of Christ (1 Corinthians 3:15), nowhere do we read that some Christians will enjoy a higher level in heaven than others.

The Book of Revelation tells us much about the eternal state of the redeemed. We read about a great multitude, which no man could number, consisting of all nations, peoples, and tongues, standing before the throne of God all clothed with white robes and saying with a loud voice: "Salvation to our God which sitteth upon the throne, and unto the Lamb" (7:9,10; see also 19:6).

13

Understanding and Dealing
With Errorists

In this last chapter we will talk about understanding and dealing with those who hold false doctrines. But before doing this, let us summarize what we have learned so far.

Review of Chapters 1 Through 12

Chapter 1. We saw that God's truth will always be under attack by Satan. Much of this work is done through groups that we call *cults*. The cults are especially dangerous because they claim to be part of the Christian church. In fact, some of them claim to be the only true Church. The most effective way to combat error is with truth—the Word of God. The Bible, and the Bible alone, is the only authority. Any group that places some other literature or tradition alongside the Bible is in error.

Chapter 2. We asked the question: "What is God like?" We saw that some people deny the existence of God; others confess they don't know whether He exists. Then there are those who say there is a God who created this world but He is no longer concerned with what goes on down here.

A number of groups teach that God is not personal, both in the sense that He himself is not a Person and that He does not take a personal interest in men. Others, like the Mormons, teach that God has a physical body. The Biblical doctrine is that God is a Spirit and He is triune. He is one God who exists and manifests himself in three Persons: the Father, the Son, and the Holy Spirit.

Chapter 3. We talked about spirit beings. The devil is a reality. He is responsible for much of the sin and heresy in the world today. But he cannot always be blamed. Sometimes sin is the result of man's own willful rebellion against God. We saw also that Satan has many helpers, whom we usually call demons or fallen angels, and that he can come as an angel of light, deceiving sincere but unsuspecting people.

Chapter 4. What is sin? Its origin was in the rebellion of Lucifer against God. But on earth its origin is attributed to Adam and Eve who willfully disobeyed God. All men have sinned; therefore, all will suffer spiritual and eternal death unless they repent and receive the Lord Jesus Christ as their Saviour.

False teachings about sin range from a denial of its existence, such as in Christian Science, to cultural relativism and situation ethics, which teach that what may be sin at one time or place may not be sin at another time or place.

Chapter 5. After talking about the reality of sin, we discussed the question: "How are we saved?" We learned that God's conditions include repentance for sin, faith in Jesus Christ, and confession of Him. Good works do not save us, but they will be the *result* of a genuine salvation experience. Water baptism will not save us, but it is a command of the Lord and must be obeyed as soon as possible after a person is saved.

Chapter 6. This dealt with teaching on the Church. We saw that the Church consists of all true believers in the Lord Jesus Christ. It exists for the threefold purpose of evangelizing the world, edifying fellow believers, and worshiping God. No one denomination can claim to be the Church in the Biblical sense. Nor does the Church have a human founder or foundation. The Lord Jesus Christ is the Rock upon which it is built.

Chapter 7. We discussed the subject of mediators. We saw that the Lord Jesus Christ, our High Priest, is the only Mediator between God and man. Also, God alone can forgive sins, contrary to the teaching of the Roman Catholic Church which places this authority in the hands of its priests.

The Bible teaches that all believers are priests in the sight of God. As priests, we first offer ourselves and our praise to God as spiritual sacrifices. Because we ourselves are priests, we do not need to go to any other human being, living or dead, to intercede for us before God. We have direct access to His presence.

Chapter 8. Here we discussed the work of the Holy Spirit. We saw that the Holy Spirit is more than an invisible force; He is a Person. His main works include regeneration or the new birth, the sanctification of God's people, and the infilling of believers by which they receive power to witness and to live for the Lord. When a person is baptized in the Holy Spirit, he will speak in tongues according to the New Testament pattern.

Chapter 9. How does God guide us? We learned that God guides us by His Word, by the Holy Spirit, by prayer, by circumstances, and by the counsel of godly, mature people. The Bible specifically condems seeking guidance by means of astrology or the occult.

Chapter 10. This dealt with the question of the security of the believer. Two extremes must be avoided. One is a complete insecurity on the part of a

Christian who does not have confidence in the Lord's ability to keep him. The other is a presumptuous attitude that says a person will remain saved regardless of the kind of life he lives.

The Bible emphasizes God's keeping power, but it also places responsibility on Christians to guard themselves spiritually. We must avoid the two extremes of fear and presumption. God's keeping power should be an encouragement to the fearful, insecure Christian. But the scriptural exhortations to abide in the Lord should be a warning to those whose lives are not glorifying God.

Chapter 11. What's ahead for the unbeliever? We examined erroneous teachings about the eternal state of the wicked. Ideas such as annihilation, a second chance, universalism, and reincarnation are all contrary to the Scriptures. The doctrine of hell as the place of eternal torment is firmly established in Scripture. But when sinful men have a wrong view of the nature of sin and the love of God, they distort the Scriptures to suit their preconceived ideas. The doctrine of hell is indeed a repugnant one. It ought to be distasteful to both sinners and Christians. But if we accept the authority of God's Word, we must accept this doctrine of eternal punishment.

Chapter 12. This dealt with the bright side of the afterlife. The Roman Catholic doctrine of purgatory is contrary to Scripture. Nowhere does the Bible say that Christians who die must undergo a time of purification before they will be worthy to enter heaven. The doctrine of soul sleep is also unscriptural. Christians do not have to wait for the resurrection of the body before they can enjoy the glories of heaven. Christians enter the Lord's presence as soon as they die.

Why Are the Cults a Threat?

Bible-believing Christians cannot close their eyes to the cults. The cults have always posed a very genuine threat to the existence of the Church. Before we can deal effectively with cultists, we must be convinced that their object is to undermine the historic Christian faith. Look at some of the reasons why they are such a threat:

1. *They are within the church.* The Christian church has always been able to deal effectively with external opposition, but most of the cults identify themselves with Christendom. In some way they claim to be followers of the Lord Jesus Christ. But many of them are really wolves in sheep's clothing.

2. *Many of them emphasize the Bible.* It is easy for unsuspecting Christians to be deceived by these cultists who seem to love the Bible so much. I remember how my family welcomed Jehovah's Witnesses into our home shortly after we were converted. Prior to that time we did not own or read the Bible. But when these visitors first came to us talking about the Bible, we felt they were doing exactly what the Lord had commanded His disciples to do. Fortunately, the Holy Spirit helped us to ask a number of questions that they could not answer. After a while they stopped coming to our home.

3. *They do not hesitate to spread their errors.* Jehovah's Witnesses and the Mormons are especially active in home visitation. Many of the cults use the printed page to considerable advantage. Some of them even sell their literature on the streets.

4. *They actively proselyte from other groups.* Many of them delight in ridiculing the historic Christian faith, pointing out how wrong the Church has always been. They do not hesitate to tell people that

they are the only ones with correct doctrine, and that you must abandon your beliefs and join their group. The cults continue to grow. Many of them, like the Mormons and Jehovah's Witnesses, are constantly making converts. Often their growth rate exceeds that of many Christian denominations.

Why Do the Cults Flourish?

It will help you to understand some of the reasons why many cults continue to attract people:

1. *Answer to human needs.* Many people who have left historic Christian churches to join a cult say that traditional Christianity did not meet their needs. They were in search of spiritual reality but did not find it in their own churches. They needed a sense of belonging or identification, and they found it in the cult they joined.

2. *Authoritativeness.* Most cults teach that they alone have the truth. They say they are the only ones who know how to interpret Scripture properly. This attitude has attracted many to their ranks. Most people are looking for someone or something to give their lives direction. Unfortunately, some do not find this in their own churches. Consequently, they are attracted to the authoritative type of cult.

3. *Aggressiveness.* It seems that anyone who is aggressive enough and persuasive enough can attract a following. Most of the cults do not hesitate to go out seeking converts, and many of their followers do so at strong, personal sacrifice.

Dos and Don'ts

How shall we deal with people who hold and teach unscriptural doctrines? Let us talk first about some things we must not do:

1. *Don't argue.* There is always a place for a calm

discussion of spiritual truth. But I have been some Christians actually lose their temper as they tried to convince someone of the error of his teachings. We must remember that the object is not to win an argument but to win a soul.

2. *Don't demonstrate a superior attitude.* Don't look down on the other person as being spiritually, intellectually, or morally inferior to yourself. Be convinced, of course, that you have and understand the truth, but do not be arrogant about it.

3. *Don't brand them as instruments of Satan.* Many of these people are sincere in their beliefs and are honestly convinced they are serving the Lord. Even though their doctrine may be satanic in origin, this does not mean they have knowingly turned themselves over to the devil.

4. *Don't make personal attacks.* It is easy to point to the shortcomings and sins of the founders and leaders of some cults. But you will not gain the attention of the person by doing this. A good rule to follow is to talk about doctrine or teachings, not about persons.

Now let us talk about how to deal with these people in a positive way:

1. *Know the facts about the other person's religion and beliefs.* You will be spared a lot of embarrassment if you restrict your comments only to what you know to be true. For instance, don't accuse a Roman Catholic of "worshiping" Mary and the saints. The official teaching of the Roman Catholic Church is that only the Trinity is to be worshiped but that it is proper to honor and pray to Mary and the saints.

2. *Use the Bible as your authority.* Many of these groups profess to accept the authority of the Bible. This is a common meeting ground you will have with

them. Be as informed as possible on the teachings of Scripture.

3. *Confess your ignorance when necessary.* If you are asked a question and you do not have the answer to it, admit it. If a cultist tries to prove a point by a certain passage of Scripture and you do not have an appropriate response, tell him you will study the matter and discuss it with him again.

4. *Be patient and loving.* Many of these people have been ensnared by false teaching. Some accepted the new doctrines at considerable personal sacrifice, and only after they studied about them for a long time. It will mean another major decision in their lives if they decide to abandon their beliefs and accept what you are saying.

5. *Be prayerful.* Allow yourself to be guided by the Holy Spirit in everything you plan to say and do as you discuss doctrinal matters with a cultist. Be prepared, but at the same time be open to the Holy Spirit's direction to guide you in saying exactly the right thing.

6. *Testify and exalt Christ.* At an appropriate time, be sure to tell these people what the Lord Jesus Christ has done for you and what He means to you. Almost always, they will not be able to testify to a personal experience of salvation or of the reality of the presence of Christ in their lives.

7. *Leave the results in the hands of God.* Have confidence in the ministry of the Holy Spirit, that after you have spoken to such a person the Lord will continue to deal with him. Perhaps your ministry will be only to sow the seed, and God will later on send someone to water it. But let us remember that the Lord is the One who gives the increase (see 1 Corinthians 3:6).